ALL ★ AROUND

and the 13th Juror

For Judy —

It's a question

of Justice —

2015 —

A Question of Justice
in the American West

ALL ★ AROUND
and the 13th Juror

Rick Steber

Cover design by Gary Asher
Page layout by Jody Conners

ISBN 978-0-945134-42-8

Other Books
by Rick Steber

Rendezvous
Traces
Union Centennial
Where Rolls the Oregon
Heartwood
Oregon Trail – Last of the Pioneers
Roundup
New York to Nome
Wild Horse Rider
Buckaroo Heart
No End in Sight
Buy the Chief a Cadillac
Legacy
Forty Candles
Secrets of the Bull
Caught in the Crosshairs
A Promise Given
Red White Black

Tales of the Wild West Series
Oregon Trail
Pacific Coast
Indians
Cowboys
Women of the West
Children's Stories
Loggers
Mountain Men
Miners
Grandpa's Stories
Pioneers
Campfire Stories
Tall Tales
Gunfighters
Grandma's Stories
Western Heroes

www.ricksteber.com

Mac Griffith
(Oregonian *newspaper, February 3, 1965)*

The 13th Juror

This true contemporary story reads like pages ripped from a dime novel. All-Around rodeo cowboy, Mac Griffith, is gunned down after a barroom brawl. The shooter is arrested and charged with murder. At the ensuing trial, a cast of truly colorful western characters parade to the witness stand. It is their testimony—what they have to say and what they are not allowed to say—that leads the jury to make its ultimate decision.

After a half-century this case is revisited, and this time those involved in the shooting tell all the graphic details of what happened, why it happened and what has played out in the aftermath. And you, the reader, have the opportunity, and perhaps the responsibility and obligation, to examine the testimony and facts of the case and come to a decision on whether a guilty man was allowed to walk free, or was the man who pulled the trigger acting within his constitutional rights when he stood his ground and took the life of another man. The final decision will be up to you, the 13th juror.

Foreword

The trial of Duane Harvey, the local man accused of murdering rodeo star, Mac Griffith, really put my hometown of Prineville, Oregon, on the map. The *Oregonian*, the state's major daily newspaper, sent a reporter as well as a sketch artist to cover the trial in Prineville. Their coverage made it seem like the fistfight and shooting could have happened in the prior century, in some Wild West town like Dodge City or Deadwood.

I was a senior at Crook County High School in 1965. My mother, Anne MacDonald, worked in the legal profession and she suggested I skip school and attend the final day of the Harvey trial. I was only too happy to oblige her. Looking back, I believe her ulterior motive was to stimulate my interest in a law career.

As I walked up the stairs to the courtroom, what struck me was the scene; it did look exactly like a set stolen from a television western; *Gunsmoke, Rawhide,* or *Have Gun Will Travel.* Men wore tall cowboy hats, work shirts and blue jeans. The judge was dressed in black and sat overlooking the courtroom while spectators, an overflow crowd, were confined to a gallery behind a classic wood railing.

Jim Bodie, the defense attorney, was a local legend at that time and represented most of the influential men in Central Oregon. He was from the Deep South and spoke with a definite twang. He was demonstrative with his choice of words and his delivery was as fire-and-brimstone as a Baptist preacher. I knew Mr. Bodie from family social gatherings and was familiar with his southern mannerisms, and on occasion, his very charming personality. But in the courtroom, all these personality traits were exaggerated and he proved to be a brilliant orator and a very convincing storyteller.

I also remember the prosecutor, a young man who seemed sadly out of place, almost lost, as he paced back and forth in front of the jury waving a derringer pistol; cocking and "dry firing" it. That struck me as a very odd thing for someone to do. From a very early age I was taught to never dry fire a gun because that wears out the firing pin.

Looking back at what transpired that day in the courtroom made me realize that "reasonable doubt" was not a widely understood concept. However, Jim Bodie made the most of "reasonable doubt" as a defense. He played up the fact the victim was a tough man and a brawler. When the verdict was read, it didn't seem as though the outcome was a particular surprise to anyone.

Having read *All-Around and the 13th Juror* I can attest to the fact the town of Prineville is accurately described. It indeed was a wild place. Fistfights were common. A lot of folks drank hard. Violent deaths came with the territory. And the trial of Duane Harvey is truthfully related. Jim Bodie was just as pompous, arrogant and flamboyant as he was portrayed. Jim Bodie, and Jim Bodie alone, decided the verdict. No doubt about that.

Tom MacDonald
Prineville, Oregon

All-Around and the 13th Juror is a masterful blend of interviews and historical research that really brings to life the town of Prineville in the early 1960s, and tells in graphic details about the shooting that occurred in the parking lot behind the Ochoco Inn. At the time of that incident, I was a freshman attending Crook County High School. My mother worked at Thrift Wise Drug Store, located in the Ochoco Inn just to the south of the Cinnabar Lounge. Mother passed on to me many of the rumors that circulated among the customers of the drug store. It seemed as though the opinion most often expressed was that the cowboy who was killed, Mac Griffith, got exactly what he had coming. Those cowboys were a rowdy bunch, as likely to fight as look at you. When the verdict was handed down, it was not a shock to anyone that the local man, Duane Harvey, was found innocent.

As a teenager, I only got bits and pieces of the story and it was hard for me to separate fact from fiction. The wonderful thing about *All-Around and the 13th Juror* is that it definitively clarifies what went on in the parking lot behind the Ochoco Inn that cold December night, as well as explaining the complicated legal process that ended with a not-guilty verdict. With publication of, *All-Around and the 13th Juror,* it is left up to the reader to decide if justice was well served in this case, or did a guilty man get away with murder.

Steve Lent
Assistant Director, Bowman Museum
Prineville, Oregon

PART ONE

The Ochoco Inn, Prineville, Oregon, circa. 1964

Cowboy Down

The Ochoco Inn, stucco skin gleaming white under incandescent lights, looks oddly out of place, as if a hacienda had been fresh plucked from Old Mexico and dropped smack dab in the middle of Oregon. It is such a magical and fabled landmark that tourists passing through Prineville—the self-proclaimed *Cowboy Capital of the World*—invariably stop to snap a photograph or two. But on this particular night in 1964, nine days shy of Christmas, the commanding façade of the Ochoco Inn visible from Third and Main streets is overshadowed by the scandalous goings-on in the parking lot behind the hotel. A cop car, red light throbbing, careens around the corner. Yellow headlights flash across the crime scene where late night revelers and gawkers stand with hands thrust in their pockets, breathing urgent clouds of warm vapor into the cold night air. This unlikely group surrounds a man lying on the ground, his head and shoulders are being cradled by a woman wearing a beige raincoat.

The car comes to an abrupt stop. The cop throws open the door, leaving it wide open and the motor running. He steps out, moving with a decisive, purposeful stride and directs the beam of his flashlight on the body of the man. What automatically catches the cop's attention is the glint of a belt buckle—depicting in sterling silver and gold a cowboy riding a bucking bull and the words *Pendleton Round-Up, All-Around Cowboy, 1963.* The distinctive buckle is worn by a big man, well-muscled, hard chiseled, brownish blond hair cropped close, handsome even, but in the glare of the harsh light his skin has taken on an ashen sheen. The woman in the raincoat who is holding him, one bare leg exposed, is crying. Her red cheeks are damp with moisture threatening to freeze.

The cop addresses the bystanders, barking, "Okay, folks, party's over. If you know anything, stick around. I'll need your statements. If not, get the hell out of here." He shuffles in the direction of the police car, moving with a deliberateness as familiar to him as the beating of his own heart, patient, but slightly harried, as if he has seen all this a hundred times and maybe he has. He reaches inside, grabs the hand mike, keys it and reports to the dispatcher, "Best get the meat wagon headed in this direction, parking lot behind the Ochoco Inn. Cowboy down: don't look good."

A capricious winter wind causes nearby trees to creak and groan; bare limbs sway, shadows scurry around and a few dry leaves skate along the ground, making a threatening buzz like a mad rattlesnake. A mill worker who has to be on the green chain pulling and stacking slabs of wet lumber in less than five hours and does not have time for statements and such tomfoolery, especially not for some goddamn rodeo cowboy, takes his hands out of his pockets, mumbles, "One dead cowboy. Hell, it's a good start." He turns and walks off into the night.

*****

The fire station is only a short block away, but it takes a good five minutes or so to rouse sufficient volunteers to man the ambulance. During this time the cop is busy gathering names and discovers the victim is none other than Mac Griffith, famous as the All-Around cowboy at the Pendleton Round-Up, and notorious among those in the law enforcement community who know him as barroom brawler and general tough guy; the kind of man a cop never wants to face without plenty of backup. But lying here, red blood staining his white shirt, blood oozing from his nose and ears, he poses absolutely no threat. His skin has turned a grayish blue and his breathing is shallow, barely enough to cause a ripple across his brawny chest. Once in a while he groans, or moans, or growls low and menacingly like a grizzly bear deep in the throes of hibernation.

The attractive woman who continues to hold the victim to her breasts is Mary Edgerly; known to the cop as a woman who frequents the local bars. Two cowboys stand nearby. They are Ronnie Raymond, from the upper country near Paulina and a past champion at the Calgary Stampede—also known to be a barroom brawler—and Jimmy Bothum, a bronc rider from St. Paul, over in the Willamette Valley. Bothum is holding his left arm close to his body. He says he injured his shoulder during the parking lot fistfight that preceded the shooting. The barmaid, Pat Leonard, joins the group. She appears to be the only sober one of the bunch.

The ambulance arrives and jockeys into position. The crew loads Mac Griffith on a stretcher, and after the ambulance roars off toward Pioneer Memorial Hospital, the cop takes the witnesses inside the Ochoco Inn and begins the arduous interviewing process. Pat Leonard resumes her post behind the bar, pours coffee for some and fresh drinks for those needing to brace themselves. The cop figures by the time he finishes writing in his black leather notebook, the truth will more than likely come out. He has already guessed the truth will not be pretty, but does not yet know the extent of all that is involved: jealousy, resentment, anger, rage, an abundance of alcohol and way too much free-flowing testosterone. What is all too obvious, the long and short of this incident, is that an unknown person brought a gun to a fistfight, and used that gun to shoot Mac Griffith.

The clock on the wall lines up on 2 a.m., limps a few minutes past, and the ringing of a telephone breaks the uncharacteristic quietness of the Cinnabar Lounge. Pat Leonard answers the phone, listens a moment and tells the cop it is for him. Upon hearing the news—Mac Griffith has been officially pronounced dead—the cop draws a deep breath to quiet his pulse. He instantly wishes he had not done such a thing. It had sounded too much like a disheartened sigh.

As the interviews progress, the cop learns the victim was a married man and had a child. He will have to notify the wife. He hates this part of his job. Maybe he can get someone else to make the call. He recognizes that Mac Griffith was a big-time star and the news of his death, like a pebble tossed into a still pond, will ripple out to touch every corner of the rodeo world. What he does not know, not yet, is that the victim had been quite a rounder, and in addition to leaving behind a wife and child, there are numerous girlfriends scattered across the Western states—one in particular, a childhood sweetheart living in Heppner—who will take the news of his passing hard, *real* hard.

In the seven weeks leading up to the trial, an Oregon State Police trainee, Larry Irwin, is fired because of his involvement in the parking lot fistfight. A Prineville mechanic, Duane Harvey, is arrested and charged with first degree murder. At his trial, Douglas Shepard, the rookie district attorney fresh out of law school, will fumble the prosecution while wily veteran defense attorney, Jim Bodie, vehemently argues Mac Griffith was nothing but an overbearing bully who got exactly what he deserved. Material witnesses are excluded from testifying. A key witness is persuaded to misrepresent the truth. Deception, distortion and even trickery are employed. The defense ultimately turns to a mesmerizing and fascinating ploy; pointing to a strange incident which occurred a continent away, in New York City. Thirty-eight people watched a woman, Kitty Genovese, being murdered in an alley and not one of those witnesses came to her aid. The jurors in the Mac Griffith case are told, *"Ladies and gentlemen of the jury, maybe murder while onlookers stand idly by is acceptable behavior in New York City, but by God, in Crook County, Oregon, it is not acceptable behavior. Here we come to the aid of our fellow man."*

PART TWO

Don and Mac Griffith
Lewiston Rodeo, circa 1949

The Brother

The Griffith family lived on a wheat, hay and cattle ranch in Kahler Basin, a dozen miles from the nearest town of Spray, Oregon. Don Griffith was 4 years older than his brother, Mac. The boys grew up riding calves and horses for entertainment. When they moved to Enterprise, Oregon, shortly after the end of World War II, the boys began competing in the sport of junior rodeo. The family moved every few years, living in La Grande, Oregon; Ephrata, Washington; Redmond, Oregon; and finally settling in Heppner, Oregon, where Mac graduated from high school in 1956.

"My little brother outgrew me in a hurry," said Don. "He was a big, strapping kid and a natural athlete. He won the All-Around at the junior rodeo in Enterprise, when he was barely 13, and won the bronc riding at the RCA rodeo in Prineville, when he was still in high school. He could pitch a rock and kill a chicken, hit it in the head every time, and could have been a hell of a professional baseball pitcher. He was that good.

"We both rodeoed. At the rodeo in Lewiston, Idaho, when I was maybe 15 and Mac was 11, we each broke our left arm in the same event, steer riding. I can't remember if we broke bones because we got bucked off, or if it was caused by trying to hang on. They gave us the *Hard Luck Trophy* for both having our left arms in slings.

"There was absolutely no quit in Mac and yet his heart was bigger than his cowboy hat. He was soft inside; loved kids. The downside for Mac was his drinking. He started when he was about 10 years old, but Mac could handle alcohol a damn site better than I ever could."

Don married Joann in 1955, but continued to rodeo with Mac on weekends. Don said, "We went to a rodeo up in Washington and Joann and I got a motel room on the second floor. Mac showed up after the bars closed. He shimmied up the drain pipe, pried the window open, threw his sleeping bag inside and slept on the floor, along with several more cowboys he invited in to stay the night. That was just the way it was in those days. Nobody was any better than anybody else.

"Mac, whether we were playing cards, drinking, fighting, riding or bulldogging, always wanted to win. He was the most determined person I've ever known. He hated to lose. I think that's why he won so often, because he was such a fierce competitor. He had determination and ability and was just beginning to scratch the surface of his potential when he was killed. He could have been the best ever.

"Mac did like to drink. When he drank he liked to fight. He was bigger and stronger than most men, but he got his ass whipped a time or two. He fought professionally in Portland and I remember him telling me, 'Those sons of bitches who box for a living can hit you whenever and wherever they want, and they make it hurt.' It didn't take Mac long to figure it out, to give up boxing and go back to the rodeo game."

Chuck Shelton, a cowboy friend, called Don in the middle of the night with the news Mac had been killed. Don did not want to believe it was true. He was stunned speechless and handed the phone to Joann to get the particulars while he packed a few clothes. He knew his mother and sisters in Heppner needed him.

As Don drove through the greenish, predawn light flooding the sagebrush and juniper country of Eastern Oregon, he was gritting his teeth at the unfairness of losing his brother. He wondered if there was anything he could have possibly done to have changed the sequence of events that ended with a bullet. He admitted this was one of his most trying moments, saying, "I didn't handle Mac's death all that well."

Duane Harvey stood trial for the murder of Mac Griffith in Prineville, and Don and the Griffith family attended. Don said, "What I remember most about the trial was the testimony of Larry Irwin, the state cop who was involved. He was an arrogant son of a bitch. It was clear from the get-go he had been schooled on what to say before he ever took the stand. I looked at him and knew there was no way in hell he could ever have whipped Mac, not in a fair fight he couldn't; not a snowball's chance in hell could he whip Mac. I think he must have had some sort of equalizer. What was it? A sap, blackjack, board? I just don't know, but it was something.

"The defense attorney, Jim Bodie, absolutely hated rodeo cowboys. To Bodie, all rodeo cowboys were thugs. He made out that my brother and his partner, Ronnie Raymond, were the worst of the lot; some sort of evil force. They had reputations as barroom fighters and Bodie used that to his advantage, twisting things around and putting Mac and Ronnie on trial. I believe the jury formed its opinion on the verdict when the district attorney, Doug Shepard, conceded in a stipulation that Mac was a troublemaker and a bully."

According to Joann Griffith, "Every day of the trial the courthouse was packed with people. The defendant's family was escorted to the courtroom, but we had to push our way up the crowded stairs. One day Don lost his temper, marched up to the sheriff and wanted to know why the Harvey family was getting special privileges, especially when the trial meant just as much to us. The sheriff seated us."

"What happened to my brother, happened a long time ago," said Don. "Most of the cowboys who knew Mac are dead and gone. I don't want to talk about it. I don't want to think about it. The fact is, Duane Harvey was a guilty man and he got away with murder. That's all there is to it."

Marilyn & Mac Griffith, Pendleton Round-Up, 1964

The Wife

Arvine Porter's 3,000 acre spread was up East Birch Creek, eight miles from the Eastern Oregon town of Pilot Rock. From all outward appearances, Arvine had it all; a substantial home ranch, a herd of cattle and hundreds of acres of leased ground planted to dryland wheat and hay. Arvine was a regular churchgoer, attending the Presbyterian Church in Pilot Rock. He seemed to have a loving and stable marriage with his high school sweetheart, Bertha—she liked to be called Bert—and their three children. The twins had come first, Gary and Larry, and then Marilyn was born three years later on October 14, 1941.

From an early age the children were expected to do chores, and summer vacations were spent riding for cattle, bucking bales and driving trucks in the wheat harvest. Just because Marilyn was a girl did not mean she had less to do. She worked alongside her brothers and grew to be a gangly girl, with long, dark hair and a very pretty face. But in the shadow of her

15

domineering father, Marilyn rarely smiled and was bashful and withdrawn. Arvine might pat one of his children on the head in passing, but he never passed out compliments or offered any sort of praise, not to his children, and certainly not to his wife. He expected dinner to be on the table whenever he came home, and the children were to have their hands and faces washed and be sitting at the table. There were no exceptions.

Marilyn claims the Porter family disintegrated when she was nine years old and the local ranchers began taking turns putting on ranch rodeos. The star of these shows became Arvine Porter. He was an expert hand with a rope, as well as a skilled steer wrestler. Marilyn recalls, "It was a fact, the ranch rodeos changed our lives. Dad got to play. We worked our tails off. Cars were parked around whatever arena it happened to be, people hanging onto the fences and having a good time, while Momma and the three of us kids ran a hot dog and hamburger stand, selling soda pop on the side.

"Dad was a big man, real handsome, and he had a personality that sparkled as bright as the sun whenever a good looking gal came around. Women certainly were attracted to my dad. They surrounded him at the rodeos. Mother called them *buckle bunnies*, and at first she tried to ignore what was going on, but something like that is a little hard for a person to just ignore. Almost overnight Dad's personality and character changed radically; he began womanizing, drinking whiskey, staying out 'til all hours, going to dances and probably doing a whole lot more than that. He quit going to church.

"Nearly every afternoon Dad would come up with some lamebrain excuse to go off alone—he was breaking a green colt, or riding for cattle—but I learned he was secretly meeting Mary Anderson, a woman from over the hill on McKay Creek. She was 12 years younger than he was and they were rendezvousing at a line cabin between the two drainages. Once again Momma tried to look the other way and ignore the obvious fact that Dad was having an affair with this woman. It made for quite the sensational scandal. All the neighbors gossiped about it. Then Mary up and left her husband and their three kids; Dad left Momma and the three of us. Those two lovebirds moved in together, onto the old Houser ranch two miles below our place. Coming or going, we had to pass the house where they were shacked up. It damn near killed Momma. She was heartbroken, but you have to hand it to her, she had nerve enough to stand up to that man. She refused to give him his divorce until he came across with the deed, free and clear, to the home ranch. A divorce wasn't an easy thing to get after the end of World War II. Momma stood her ground, even when Mary went to town and legally changed her last name from Anderson to Porter. There for a while Dad and Mary's ex-husband, Red, were both packing guns. Dad and Mary eventually had two children of their own, and if he wanted his divorce, Dad had to give Momma the deed, and he did.

"For us kids, all during this whole ugly mess of having two families ripped apart, we were still expected to hike the two miles to Dad's new place and do chores and work for him. Nothing had changed on that front.

"The summer I was 13, I got it in my head I wanted a squaw dress. They were the popular thing to wear, and I went to Dad and asked if he would buy me a squaw dress. He said he'd have to check with Mary. I was mad at that and rebelled, wanting to know, 'What's she got to do with it?' When Dad failed to answer, I gave him the second barrel, 'I've worked since school let out and I deserve that dress.' The next day he informed me Mary had been wanting a squaw dress and he hadn't bought her one, so no, I couldn't have my squaw dress.

"That was all I could take. I called my Aunt Helen in Pendleton and she came and got me. Aunt Helen had a big three-story house at 511 Despain Avenue, and her husband, George Stangier, owned a lot of downtown property, including the Temple Hotel. He had money and position in the community. Aunt Helen put me to work at 50 cents an hour doing housework, running errands, ironing, mowing the lawn and working in the yard. Every afternoon I was granted a couple hours to go to the public pool to swim and cool off. That summer I had the best tan ever.

"I had to go home when school started. What did I learn from that experience with my father, really *all* my experiences with my father? I learned hate and resentment will slowly eat a person alive. Did I develop wounds and scars at a relatively young age? Yes, I did. Did I resent never having had my father tell me he loved me, being cuddled, and feeling safe and protected? I resented the hell out of it. Then I turned around, met Mac Griffith, married him, and he was the exact same man as my dad, the one person I was trying so desperately to get away from."

*****

Marilyn was 15 years old the summer Arvine hired two strapping young fellows from the neighboring town of Heppner, 40 miles away, to work in the haying. One was Freddie Livingstone and the other was Mac Griffith. Marilyn knew nothing about the two. They showed up in a pickup truck and the ranch dogs came out to bark at the new arrivals. Freddie reached out to pet one of the dogs and drove him mistrustfully off. But Mac, with knowledgeable casualness, crawled out from behind the wheel, allowed one hand to hang knuckles forward, the dog sniffed, and Mac scratched the animal accommodatingly behind its ears.

Mac had already graduated from Heppner High School, where he was a star football player at running back, and a champion bronc and bull rider on the amateur rodeo circuit. Later Marilyn would learn of his reputation as a tough boy, a brawler who never backed away from a fight, never in his life.

That first day of work, the boys were bucking hay bales onto the bed of the truck where Arvine was stacking. Marilyn drove the old International truck, and as she zigzagged between bales, Mac was riding her hard, telling her to speed up, saying he and Freddie were going to swamp her old man with hay. Arvine fell behind, and the bales piled up waiting to be stacked. Arvine, sweating profusely, had to admit he couldn't keep up, rapping a hay hook on the cab of the truck and yelling at Marilyn to slow down. By then the boys' shirts had been discarded and Marilyn found her gaze drifting in the direction of Mac Griffith. She noticed his slender waist, broad shoulders and the way the muscles across his chest and up and down his shoulders and arms rippled and flexed. Her young mind leaped a guilty mile and she thought, if he offered to kiss her on a sudden impulse, or a sharp stab of adolescent affection, she would not—could not—resist.

Mac started to lift a bale, but hesitated just long enough to flash a grin and throw a teasing wink in Marilyn's direction. Her eyes flickered in embarrassment and her lips puckered and pursed. She hoped to God Mac had not seen that, and had only seen her frosty frown that followed.

After that brief exchange, Marilyn drove between the rows of bales single-mindedly avoiding any eye contact with Mac while mulling the obvious notion that he was quite capable of drawing any girl's attention. The skin on his neck, face and arms, from mid-bicep down, was a weather-beaten brown. His hair was close cropped and fine, but already beginning to thin some at his temples. He moved with an air of confidence, not so much walking but more like effortlessly floating across the hayfield. He kept his head down, looking at the ground; lower lip thrust forward in a mocking scowl or as a sign of pure aggression. Marilyn began questioning her newfound emotions, questioning what it was about Mac that drew her interest. Was it his physical appearance? Yes. The way he swaggered with the confidence of a young man who knew he was good looking? Yes. Could there be something more to it? More than likely what appealed to Marilyn the most was Mac's *anything goes* attitude and the way he had challenged Arvine Porter to a hay-hauling contest and whipped him. Now she studied Mac and noticed his mouth. When he was not grinning and clowning around, viewed from the side, his profile gave the appearance of sadness. Perhaps he was privy to an insight, could see off into the future and what he saw worried and depressed him.

The lethal heat of the day remained long into the night. Marilyn lay on her bed in her pajamas, pulling and coaxing the thin material away from her sticky skin. She glanced toward the screened window, optimistically hoping for a breeze, but between slack curtains gaped a night too close and stifling to flow. Marilyn smelled the pungent odors of curing hay and warm, decaying ground. She felt a claustrophobic sense that the walls were closing in around her, and as a distraction picked up a nail file and immediately set it back down on the night stand. She snapped off the light. Her moist skin contracted in erratic goose bumps as will sometimes occur when a body enters a pond secretly after dark during a heat wave; when the water and air are nearly the same temperature and the passage from air to water is hardly more than the rapid change from the pull of gravity to the rush of buoyancy. In that moment, Marilyn experienced images of Mac in the hayfield, flashing like a series of washed-out black and white photographs lacking in any solid details. She licked her dry lips and waited for sleep, but sleep was a reluctant visitor that night.

A fresh new day began under a cloudless sky. Marilyn came fully awake, vaulted from bed, jumped into her work clothes and hurried through breakfast with a single thought in mind—to see Mac as quickly as possible.

*****

One Saturday, after evening chores were finished, Mac suggested that maybe Marilyn would like to go to the picture show in Pendleton. She stood in front of him and defiantly said, "Not if you're wearing that ten-gallon hat, I'm not. I'd die of embarrassment."

Mac's eyes narrowed and he squinted at her like an old woman trying to find the eye of a needle in dim light. The squinting regard persisted until, as if a signal had been given, he changed his demeanor and smiled brightly. He shrugged his burly shoulders and drawled, "Suit yourself, 'cause I'm wearin' my hat, darlin'." Mac was stubborn that way, never gave any room for a compromise, and did exactly what he wanted to do. That night he wore his hat, and before he and Marilyn could get out of the driveway, Gary and Larry came running out and piled into the pickup. They roared off toward Pendleton.

*****

Marilyn was in her junior year of high school and Mac, when he was not riding in Rodeo Cowboy Association (RCA) sanctioned rodeos in small towns around the Northwest, drove his pickup truck to Pilot Rock to take Marilyn to a movie and sometimes accompany her to a school dance or a ball game. Even though Marilyn heard the rumors that Mac had a girlfriend in Heppner, Sharon Bryant, and was a popular cowboy with the *buckle bunnies* on the rodeo circuit, it didn't seem to matter much because she was confident Mac liked her best.

Mac went to work logging in the Ochoco Mountains, a hundred miles away, and still he showed up in Pilot Rock a couple times a month. The summer before Marilyn's senior year of high school, Mac showed up unexpectedly and they went for a drive up Bear Creek Road. Mac bragged, "Between logging during the week, and riding rodeos on the side, I'm making pretty good money."

He pulled into a turnout, cut the engine and they just sat in silence. Mac could oftentimes be sullen, moody and quiet. Marilyn studied a male mountain quail as it strolled from the brush along the side of the road, hopped onto the low branch of an elderberry and walked the horizontal tightrope. His vest was a vivid slate blue, his belly was patterned like rusty links of chain link fence, his throat and eyebrows were outlined in white, his back a flat gray and his plume bobbed jauntily over one eye. Behind him came a plump, self-satisfied female that hopped onto the same limb as the male. The male paused to peck at a knot on the limb, and the devoted female, following, stopped and pecked the same knot. The pair disappeared into the leaves and a moment later three bright notes sounded, "er, er, errr," with the last note slurring downward like the perfect exclamation point at the end of a long-winded sentence.

21

Marilyn squirmed even closer to Mac and momentarily rested her head on his shoulder in an intentional show of affection. Mac remained aloof, as sullen as a sick dog. His eyebrows were arched. Marilyn wanted to jokingly offer him a penny for his thoughts, but refrained. What Marilyn did not know was that Mac's high school girlfriend in Heppner, Sharon Bryant, had married a local farmer, Kenny Cutsforth. And now Mac was sitting along this country road contemplating his options. He and Sharon had gone together through his last two years of high school and he fancied her. But now she belonged to another man. He thought about Sharon and the girls he met at rodeos, good-time girls good for one night and quickly discarded. Mac abruptly reached up, gripped the steering wheel with both hands, and without ever looking in Marilyn's direction he said, "I don't want to go on living without you. Why don't you move up to Fossil with me? We'll get a place in town. We can get married. What do you say?"

Marilyn didn't know what to say, what to think. Her mouth was dry and her thoughts labored. A thin wire of a headache skewered from one temple to the other as she contemplated becoming Mac Griffith's wife. There were plenty of reasons to reject his offer. She was too young, needed to finish high school before she even thought of marriage, and she had planned to go to secretarial or beauty school. She knew she should establish a career for herself rather than be dependent on a man. But overriding any reasonable thinking was the simple fact Mac represented freedom to Marilyn, a way to escape from home and the oppressive domination of her father.

"Don't wear out your brain," laughed Mac. He had turned and was facing Marilyn. "Just say yes. Say you'll be my wife."

A sharp quiver raced through Marilyn like a spear stuck humming into a tree. She was caught between returning his smile, saying yes, or meeting him head-on with a scowl and a definite no. Her hands clenched and unclenched in her lap. She did not seem to possess enough tension in her body to move her lips; much less have the wind necessary to vibrate her vocal cords. When she did speak it was as if the single word was emerging from a muted horn. She said, "Yes." And just as soon as she had voiced that word, a pang of doubt caused her smile to dissipate. Then he kissed her.

Mac was full of himself as he confidently twisted the key and started the pickup truck. It coughed, sputtered and caught. He popped the clutch and the rig rolled forward with a protesting lurch, banging into and out of potholes in the road and crunching gravel as they headed toward town.

*****

Marilyn had informed her mother she was getting married, and now in the gray light of afternoon, the tall grandfather clock that sat in the corner of the room went on steadily measuring time. It was not so much time it measured as the distance its pendulum swung. The hands could be torn off the face and the brass bob would continue its solemn beat as steady as the wings of a pelican in flight; its ominous ticking pretending to have meaning, the clock striking every hour, loud chimes booming through the room, but the hands never moving. Marilyn's mother, Bert, said nothing. There was just that irritating tick-tick-tick to break the threatening silence.

Bert stared out the window. A breeze had come from somewhere and the light underbellies of the leaves on the locust tree riffled, shivered silver and then returned to somber green. Bert wanted to express her misgivings about Mac Griffith, but did not know how to put into words that, in her opinion, Mac seemed to be missing some essential human quality, something vital, like pigment missing from the skin of an albino, or the fact that white horses are prone to blindness. She had heard rumors of Mac's many girlfriends, his frequent fistfights, and had watched him compete at rodeos. When Mac rode he was wild and unpredictable, throwing caution to the wind. He came out spurring and never quit until after the animal had been subdued, and even then he sometimes pushed an animal past the breaking point. Bert did not want to take the chance of allowing Mac to break her daughter's spirit. Bert was feeling a mother's responsibility, trying to protect her daughter from harm, from making a bad decision, from ruining her life.

In a voice as dry and whirring as the gears of that grandfather clock, her eyes hard-set and unyielding, Bert broke the unhealthy quiet and said, "Honey, he's just not right for you. You need to finish school. If you marry him, mark my words, you'll live to regret it. Wait until you're 18. I won't sign for you."

"Fine," said Marilyn, abruptly standing and defiantly walking away, tossing over her shoulder, "No worry. Dad will sign."

Arvine Porter did sign the legal document giving his consent and allowing his underage daughter to marry Mac Griffith. Arvine and Bert did not attend the June 13, 1958 wedding of Marilyn and Mac. They were not invited.

The bride and groom moved to the small town of Fossil, Oregon, where they lived in an unfurnished apartment. The only furniture in the place was a mattress on the floor. Marilyn wanted more, and Mac promptly withdrew $500 from savings and took Marilyn to Portland to shop for furniture. Mac worked during the week for John Hudspeth's logging crew, bumping knots, cutting limbs off logs with a power saw. It was hard, dirty work, but Mac never complained.

That fall, when the snow came and shut the loggers out of the woods, the young couple moved to a remote ranch where Mac fed hay to a herd of cattle every morning and again in the afternoons. Marilyn recalls, "Those were the best days of our lives. We didn't have electricity. We used kerosene lamps. We didn't have indoor plumbing. We had an outhouse. Sometimes in the evenings we played board games or cards. We read books. Mac loved westerns, but he was a slow reader. Reading was difficult for him. Even if we were doing nothing, we had fun. We talked a lot that winter. Mac told me about his growing-up years. The Griffiths had lived on a hard-scrabble ranch in the hills north of the town of Spray. When Mac was maybe 6 years old the family moved to Northeastern Oregon, to Enterprise, and Mac and his brother, Don, started riding at junior rodeos.

They had a lot of natural talent and did well. One thing Mac told me was that his father was a hard drinker, and when he came home from a binge, the boys had to hide their mother or their dad would beat her. At that point of our lives, for Mac, drinking was not an issue. We didn't have a bottle in the house and we were snowbound and couldn't go anywhere."

*****

As far back as high school, Mac proved himself to be a scrapper. He was quick with his hands, had power in his punches and was tough and mean. Although he never went out of his way to pick a fight, he was eager to be the one who finished a fight. He earned a well-deserved reputation as a brawler and all of Mac's friends knew any time a fight broke out they could always count on Mac to back them up.

The winter Mac spent feeding out, he got it in his head he could become a professional fighter and make easy money in the ring. He put the furniture in a storage shed at Arvine's place, loaded Marilyn in his pickup truck and they drove to Portland where they rented a furnished apartment. During the days, Mac worked for Waco Scaffolding Company, putting up and tearing down scaffolding. In the afternoons and evenings, he trained at an eastside gym with former World Middleweight Champion, Carl "Bobo" Olson.

Marilyn detested the gym. It smelled of sour sweat and dreams that would never come true. While Mac trained she usually stayed in the apartment watching television on the black and white set. It was the first television she had seen. Mac took time off every once in a while and he and Marilyn made a night of it, going to a movie or having dinner at a restaurant. Mac, in training, had given up drinking and was supposed to give up smoking too—he smoked unfiltered Camels and sometimes Lucky Strikes—but he was never able to kick the habit and smoked on the sly. Other than his addiction to cigarettes, Mac took his training seriously, and got up early every morning to run in a nearby park.

Mac's first professional fight was against a journeyman boxer. Although Mac was a great brawler, he was not a boxer. Marilyn sat in the stands and watched in horror as her husband took a beating. She recalled, "Mac led with his face and the other man just stepped to one side or the other and peppered Mac with punches, cutting up his face something terrible. Mac got knocked down several times, but always got to his feet before the referee counted him out. I prayed for him to stay down. But he kept getting up. It seemed like the fight went on forever. I couldn't watch and put my face in my hands and cried."

Mac's career lasted only three professional fights. He was knocked down in each of the fights, but was never counted out. Three beatings convinced Mac he would never become a skilled boxer. He gave up the sport and he and Marilyn moved to Salem, Oregon, where Mac attempted to sell vacuum cleaners and sewing machines door-to-door. He was only slightly more successful as a salesman than he had been as a boxer. Behind on rent, with creditors constantly calling, Mac returned to what he was best at, rodeo, and moved with Marilyn to Pendleton.

Mac rodeoed on weekends, and during the week he worked for Arvine Porter at the Pendleton bar he had purchased, the Olympia. Mac was a bartender, part-time bouncer and ran the poker game in the back room. According to one story, there was an altercation in the Olympia involving a drunken Indian. Mac stepped in, hit the Indian so hard he knocked the man completely out of his boots and into the street.

"Mac didn't drink during the day, nor did he when he worked, but most every evening he partied. He partied hard," said Marilyn. "I think it was Mark Twain who said something to the effect that every man is a moon and has a dark side that he doesn't let anyone see. But everyone saw Mac's dark side. It was his drinking. When he drank his personality totally changed. He became a different person, a stranger really, and at the drop of a hat could go from this carefree and fun-loving guy to someone I didn't even know—aggressive and confrontational. Some nights he came home with the knuckles on his hands swollen and bleeding and I'd ask what had happened, but he never gave me a straight answer. Sometimes I went along for the ride, to the bars around Pendleton, and Mac would get a few beers under his belt and switch to whiskey, drinking it with Coke or water. I don't think Mac ever went into a bar with the intention of getting into a fistfight, but when you're in a crowded bar someone is going to bump you, step on your foot, spill a drink, look at you the wrong way, and that's what starts a fight. Rarely was it Mac's fight, but he had a way of stepping into his friends' fights. Mac had a lot of friends. When the fists started flying it was Katie bar the door. The last person standing was usually Mac. Boxing might not have been his forte, but barroom brawls certainly were.

"Mac's fighting didn't bother me all that much. But Mac's lovin' side did bother me. If Mac had a snoot full he might very well walk away, leave me standing alone in the middle of the barroom, and take up with some other gal. He would be hugging and kissing on her right out in the open in front of me. He never tried to hide it. He didn't give a good goddamn how it made me feel.

"One time I went with Mac to a rodeo in Reno, Nevada. We stopped at a casino. Mac played blackjack and I played the nickel slot machines. We set a time to meet, but Mac was a no-show. I went looking and found him in the bar snuggled up with one of the cocktail waitresses. She was all but falling out of her skimpy outfit. Mac had his chair pulled up next to her and was nuzzling her neck. Mac was like that when he was drinking and he was good enough looking he got away with it. Mac did what Mac wanted to do, when he wanted to do it, and nobody—especially not me—was supposed to object. That day in the casino he just looked at me like I didn't exist and kept horsing on the cocktail waitress. I should have left him high and dry, but I went back to our hotel room and waited."

*****

Mac joined the Rodeo Cowboy Association (RCA), and if he had the entry fees he typically competed in five events: bull riding, saddle bronc, bareback, bulldogging and calf roping. When he rode, he was reckless and wild, taking chances and riding to win. If he bucked off, he merely set his sights on the next event, or the next rodeo on down the line. He traveled with men like Marty Wood, three times World Saddle Bronc Champion, Ronnie Raymond, Saddle Bronc Champion at the Calgary Stampede and Jimmy Bothum, an up-and-coming bronc rider from the Willamette Valley. The men rode tough, traveled fast and partied hard.

"Mac was the kind of man who never should have gotten married," said Marilyn. "He wanted the comfort of having a wife to come home to, and yet when he walked out the door he saw himself as free-wheeling and fancy free. That's the way he swung. No responsibilities, no cares.

"Paying entry fees, traveling and partying took a lot of money and Mac seldom sent anything home to me. When I couldn't pay my rent on our house in Pendleton, the only choice I had was to move home and live with Mom. That was a hard pill for me to swallow. And Mom, never one to mince words, told me straight out that Mac felt no sense of responsibility, no obligation to support me. She said I better find a way to support myself. Bless her kind heart, Mom had saved her money and offered to pay my tuition to Pendleton College of Beauty. She wanted me to have a career to fall back on. I enrolled at the beauty school and lived with Aunt Helen."

*****

Mac was busy chasing his dream, winning rodeos and garnering fame. He won the bulldogging championship at Pendleton as well as the All-Around. He won at Calgary, Chicago and Cheyenne. It was said he was a cinch to win the World All-Around title. He lived a dangerous life in the rodeo arena, on the road and in the bars. And when the bars closed he often called Marilyn and sometimes Marilyn would be cranky and ask, "Why are you calling me? Couldn't you find some gal to shack up with you for the night?"

Mac might say, "I sleep with whatever gal lets me in her bed, but you're the one I love, Honey." He would profess his love and Marilyn usually cried. The calls in the middle of the night were disturbing, and became such a nuisance that Aunt Helen told Marilyn she had to leave. Marilyn moved in with a girlfriend, Betty Pedro, but Mac found out where she was and the late night phone calls resumed.

"Mother told me to take the blinders off; that Mac was never going to be there for me," said Marilyn. "I got up the nerve to file for divorce. Mac even went with me to see our family attorney, Ralph Currin, and have him draw up the papers. Mac told Ralph to give me whatever I asked for. Mac was so apologetic and sincere that day—acting like he really did have feelings for me and care about my well-being—that I never followed through with the divorce. I have a sneaking suspicion Mac doubled back and told Ralph to put things on hold. Anyway, no official papers were ever served.

"Even though I might not have been legally divorced, I felt as though Mac had abandoned me and I was free to explore my options. I dated a few men, nobody seriously. There was one fellow from Hermiston, Bob, a nice guy, and I went out with him several times. When Round-Up rolled around Mac came to town, and although I never knew this at the time, Mac found out about Bob and beat him up. All I ever knew was Bob just stopped calling me.

"Whenever Mac was in town he wanted me to go drinking with him, and what invariably happened was we ended up in bed. I knew I shouldn't be doing what I was doing, but I was powerless to stop it. Mac was my addiction.

"Mac and I were together over the Fourth of July. A couple weeks later I was visiting Mom and was sick to my stomach. I thought I had come down with the flu. Mom took one look at me, shook her head and announced, 'I know what's wrong with you. You're pregnant.'"

*****

In 1963 Mac won the bulldogging at the Calgary Stampede, and followed that by winning the bulldogging and All-Around title at the Pendleton Round-Up. He was in the money, and in the mood to celebrate. Marilyn said, "I went out with Mac the night he won the Round-Up. He picked me up in a brand new Oldsmobile 98, a pretty car, white with white leather interior. He asked me how I liked my new car and told me the title was registered in my name. What was I supposed to think? It wasn't like I was going to be driving that car, and when Mac was finished with it in a year or two, it would have a couple of hundred thousand miles on it and be a pile of junk.

"Of course we hit the bars that night and everyone wanted to congratulate Mac. He was the shining star, the golden local boy who had made it to the big time. With Mac it was hard to tell when he was drunk because he was never sloppy, staggering, or slurring his words. But I knew Mac was over his limit when we ran into Harry Charters in a downtown bar. Harry was a mountain of a man, standing six-foot-six and weighing over 250 pounds. He was an accomplished roper and bulldogger, probably Mac's main competitor on the circuit. He stepped up to congratulate Mac on his win, stuck out his hand and what did Mac do? He threw his drink in Harry's face. The fight could have been on and the two of them would have torn up the place. But Harry, always the gentleman, walked away. I admired Harry for doing that.

"I knew before the evening was over Mac was going to end up in jail, so I took him back to my apartment. The next morning Mac rolled out of bed, pulled on his clothes and announced he was going uptown to play poker with friends. Three days later he called me from Heppner, to say how much he loved me and that he had to see me again. He acted as though he had just run down to the grocery store to grab a loaf of bread and a gallon of milk. But the moccasin telegraph works fast in Pendleton. I knew Mac was in Heppner, spending time with his mother, and his old girlfriend, Sharon Bryant. I told Mac I had had it with him and to stay the hell away from me. And since he had me pissed off, I went ahead and told him I was pregnant. He didn't react like I thought he would. He was thrilled, absolutely thrilled. He made me a lot of promises that day; said he was going to be a better man, give up his old ways and settle down. He promised he was going to be a real father to our baby. Promises. Promises. Promises."

*****

For a while Mac did make an effort to alter his behavior. He frequented the bars less often and went out of his way to avoid trouble. He focused on his riding, bulldogging and roping and his improved performances led to wins and accolades. It appeared as though Mac truly did have a legitimate shot at winning the top prize, the World All-Around title. But the inertia of his lifestyle was a difficult thing for Mac to change over a sustained period and gradually he fell back into his old ways.

Marilyn graduated from beauty school, and then because of her difficult pregnancy, she moved in with her mother. Marilyn suffered with constant nausea. The only thing she could keep down was oatmeal. Sometimes she ate oatmeal morning, noon and night.

Mac was proud of his impending fatherhood, and even though the event was still months away, he carried around a shirt pocket full of fat cigars with the announcement, "It's A Boy!" printed on the cellophane wrapper. He handed them out to his friends at the rodeos.

*****

"The only time I ever saw Mac scared was the night he saw a vision, or God, or whatever it was he saw, but he definitely saw something." said Marilyn. "Mac was home between rodeos. We drove to Heppner, to visit his mother, Eva."

Eva lived on Willow Street, the last house on the block, tucked up tight against the sharp incline of a ridge. A few blocks away was the Heppner United Methodist Church with a tall white steeple adorned with three black crosses. Mac cut the engine and he and Marilyn sat in the dark in front of his mother's house, just talking. The dash lights were on, a crescent moon was shining down and the stars were out. Whenever she turned her head, tiny bursts of light winked on and off from Marilyn's earrings. Music played softly on the radio. The night was still. They talked about nothing in particular; were just visiting about friends and family.

"Mac gave a sudden gasp," said Marilyn, "and grabbed hold of the wheel like the car was spinning out of control. But we weren't moving. His body went rigid, eyes wide open, the vein on his forehead bulged, pounded, and he had this intense, faraway look like I had never seen.

"I snapped, 'What's wrong?' He didn't answer, just stared straight ahead and kept that death grip on the steering wheel. 'Mac, are you alright?' I asked, but I knew he wasn't alright. That much was obvious. The lighting wasn't good and yet it seemed to me Mac had gone white as a ghost.

"When Mac broke his silence, his words were flat, lifeless, monotone. He asked, 'Do you see it?'

"I looked where he was looking, saw nothing but the night, the moon shadows and the church spire with the three crosses. 'See what?' I asked, taking hold of his right arm. His bicep muscles were bunched as hard as a knot. He let out a breath, a gasp really. I could feel his heart hammering in his chest. He was sweating, taking quick, urgent gulps of air and expelling them hard and fast. I thought something traumatic was happening; he was having a seizure, stroke, heart attack.

"Then he began describing what he was seeing, choosing his words carefully, taking his time. Mac said, 'He's wearing this flowing white robe. A cloud floats around him, a cloud of fire. He looks at me. His eyes are yellow, red, blue; like burning embers.'

"He broke away from this vision, turned to me, begged me to say I could see this thing—what he was seeing—I could not. He looked back at whatever it was and groaned as if the sight made him sick to his stomach.

"I shouted, 'Start this goddamn car! Get the hell out of here!' And he turned the key, dropped the transmission in gear and we tore away with tires spinning and gravel flying. He stopped downtown at the bar and got out, never said one word until we were inside and then he ordered a whiskey, a double straight up. He hadn't had a thing to drink all day, but he tossed down that drink in one gulp. That seemed to settle his nerves. He closed his eyes. His breathing became more normal. His heart was no longer beating a mile a minute. Tears moistened his eyes. He wiped them away and tried to explain what he had seen. He said, 'It was a human form, but it didn't seem human. It was a man wrapped in a sheet. He had white hair and a white beard that flowed down to the center of his chest. He was standing in this ball of fire, flames swirled around him. He moved slowly. He came toward me. Maybe it was God. I don't know.' He paused, seemed to gather himself and continued. 'Those eyes—so intense—staring at me, through me, burning into me. I don't know. I can't explain it. I saw what I saw. It was real. You didn't see it, did you?'

"I shook my head. Mac fell silent once again. I motioned to the bartender to bring him another. When it came, Mac sat hunched over it, elbows on the table, those big hands of his cradling the glass, clenching it. Mac was trying to clear his head of the disturbing vision, or at least to make some kind of sense of it, but he couldn't and I said, 'If what you saw was God, maybe He was trying to tell you something. Take stock of the way you're living. Ask yourself if you're the man you want to be. Have you been the best husband you could be? Will you be the father our baby needs you to be?" I allowed my hands to drop to my belly for emphasis. My pregnancy was showing.

"When Mac did respond I wasn't sure he had heard what I said. He turned to me with his eyes glazed over. His bottom lip drooped and quivered. The best way I could describe the expression on his face is to say he looked empty. His voice was lifeless, devoid of any trace of emotion, as if he was speaking from a deep sleep, or a trance. He somberly said, 'I'll be dead before I'm 30. Dead before I'm 30.'"

*****

Had Mac witnessed a disturbing apparition, or was it more sinister? Had he caught a glimpse of his own death? Had he suffered a brain aneurism, a bleeding in his brain caused by the accumulative effects of the blows he had absorbed in brawls, in the boxing ring and from his wild rides on the rodeo circuit? The truth would never be known. But the unsettling hallucination did trigger a positive reaction in Mac. He cut back on his drinking, fought less, and when around home he was a more attentive husband to Marilyn.

Mac was riding high, ranked in the top ten money winners in the RCA standings for the World All-Around Champion. It was Mac who suggested that Marilyn accompany him to the rodeo in Las Vegas. She was still nauseous from her pregnancy, but convinced herself it would be a fun outing, and Mac had so seldom asked her to ride with him that she threw caution to the wind.

It was a long, exhausting drive and when they arrived in Las Vegas and checked into the hotel, Marilyn knew she had made a mistake. Mac suggested they go out on the town. But all Marilyn could do was lie in bed and try to rest. When she felt up to it, she rang room service and ordered oatmeal and dry toast. That was what she could keep down.

For three days and nights Mac never once returned to the hotel room, not to check on Marilyn, to take a shower, or grab a change of clothes. It was not until after the rodeo was over, sometime in the middle of the night, that Marilyn awoke to find Mac dropping his boots on the floor, slipping out of his pants and shirt and socks and sliding into bed with her.

"He came slithering over to my side like a snake through the grass," said Marilyn. "I didn't want anything to do with him. I did not speak, did not fly off the handle or kick him where I had every right to kick him. Any man who treats a woman—especially a woman who is going to be the mother of his child— like Mac treated me, was not someone I wanted to be with. I was royally pissed and scooted to the far side of the bed, as far away from him as I could get. But Mac wanted to get romantic. He whispered he loved me and tried to touch me. I snapped, 'Don't you dare! Keep your hands to yourself.' He lay there for a moment and then his body began to shake. He was breathing hard. He grunted, 'I'm having a heart attack.' And I told him he could damn well go ahead and have a heart attack, but if he was going to flop around like a fish tossed on the bank, he better have his heart attack on the floor. That's exactly what I told him.

"I never though for a minute Mac was really having a heart attack. What I figured was he had a bad case of guilty conscience; probably from running off with some lady friend and leaving me, in my condition to fend for myself. I was so exhausted, and I suppose relieved he was back, I fell asleep. When I awoke, Mac was up, showered and shaved, had on clean clothes and was ready to roll. When we went downstairs he made a spectacle of himself by telling anyone and everyone within earshot that he had the best woman in the world. I was the perfect wife and I was going to have his baby. I wasn't buying any of Mac's bullshit. So why did I stay with a man like that? I do not know. Young and foolish explains it. That and the only other example I had of how a man was supposed to act was my father. Hell, I didn't know any better."

*****

Mac was on the road chasing the RCA All-Around title when Melinda "Mindy" Griffith was born on March 12, 1964. It was three weeks before Mac got home and held his baby in his arms. When she was born, Mac was teased unmercifully by his cowboy friends for having handed out "It's a Boy!" cigars. Even though Mac wanted a boy, once he held Mindy, he took a real shine to her. The times he did make it back to Pilot Rock, the first thing he wanted to do was to hold Mindy and play with her. He was a doting father.

But Mac was kept busy traveling from one rodeo to the next. As summer slipped into fall, Mac planned one last big push to move up in the standings by making a swing to the East Coast and the large paydays at the rodeos in Toronto, New York, Boston, Chicago and St. Louis before ending the year at the Western Championship Finals Rodeo in Victorville, California.

Mac was driving his white Oldsmobile 98 when he swung into the town of Prineville to pick up a couple of cowboys to travel with him; Ronnie Raymond and Jim Bothum. They met at the local watering hole, the place where cowboys gathered, the Cinnabar Lounge at the Ochoco Inn. It was here Mac cashed a hundred dollar check on a closed account, and when the check bounced, papers were filed with the circuit court and a trial date was scheduled for December 15, 1964.

The letter notifying Mac of his required court appearance was sent to Bert's address, the address listed on Mac's driver's license. When Mac got home from his East Coast trip he told Marilyn the court appearance was just a misunderstanding, no big deal, a mistake and nothing more. After all, he was Mac Griffith and he reasoned when he blew into Prineville, fresh off of winning the All-Around title, any minor problem with a bad check would certainly be forgiven. That was what he told Marilyn.

*****

The Pacific International Livestock Exposition (PI) rodeo was going on and Mac Griffith was sitting pretty, tied for first place in the bull riding competition. He called Marilyn and invited her to come over. She borrowed her mother's car and drove to Portland. Marilyn recalled, "I walked in with Mindy and Mac gave me a quick kiss, took Mindy and paraded around with her, showing her off, and then took her into the bar. He was in Seventh Heaven."

In addition to his success in bull riding, Mac was also in the finals of the saddle bronc competition. His buddy, Jim Bothum, led in points, with Ronnie Raymond riding a close second. Mac sat in third. The friends celebrated their good fortune by drinking. Mac tried to encourage Marilyn to stay and party with them, but Mindy was showing signs of colic, and Marilyn, disgusted that Mac could not recognize the fussing and discomfort Mindy was exhibiting in the smoky environment, took her baby to Mac's hotel room and waited. When Mac did roll in, a new day was breaking. All he had time for was to pack his bags, plant quick kisses on Marilyn and Mindy, and he was off down the road with his traveling partners.

"That was Mac," said Marilyn with a sad shake of her head. "He was a lively whirlwind who touched down here, and there, and somewhere else. On the drive back to Pilot Rock I was feeling sorry for myself. I knew Mac had money in his pocket—not that he had shared any of it with me, not even gas money—and now he was off chasing the World All-Around Cowboy title. While he led the high life, I was expected to stay home and be the perfect wife and mother. Some of it was the *Leave it to Beaver* mentality of the times we were living in, but some of it was Mac too. What did I have? All I had was an insecure future with a rodeo cowboy, and a colicky baby in need of my constant attention; a hell of a life."

Mac maintained his winning ways, capturing the Canadian Championship and earning paydays at most of the big rodeos. His year was down to the finals in Los Angeles, and then he would be home to spend the holidays with Marilyn and Mindy at Bert's house on the ranch out of Pilot Rock.

"I wanted Mindy's first Christmas to be something special," said Marilyn. "Mom and I put up a tree, decorated it, and even though we didn't have much money I splurged on toys and special outfits for Mindy.

"Mac hadn't done as well as he had wanted at the Western Championship Finals Rodeo, but there were no more rodeos and he came home to Pilot Rock. I was really looking forward to having him around and had convinced myself this would be a special time for us to try and be a family. It may sound crazy, but I saw this as an opportunity for us to try and make our marriage work. I knew Mac loved me, and he loved his baby, but he was just never around. Now we would all be together for a few weeks and maybe Mac would decide he liked home life better than he liked the road."

Mac drove in from California to Bert's house on the home ranch. He got in late, spent the night with Marilyn and got up early the next morning, making coffee and mixing pancakes from a box of Aunt Jemima's. He poured maple syrup over the stack and ate while the few remaining birds sang outside in the trees.

When Marilyn awoke she ran a hairbrush through her hair, brushed her teeth, changed Mindy's diapers and came to the kitchen to see what Mac was doing. He took Mindy and set her on his lap. As he played with Mindy he told Marilyn he was heading to Prineville to make his court date on Wednesday morning. He said it would be a quick trip. He would pay his fine and probably be home Wednesday night.

"I asked him where he was staying," said Marilyn. "I knew he would stay at the Ochoco Inn. He always did. I made him promise he wouldn't go to the bar. I said if he went to the Cinnabar and started drinking, there was bound to be trouble. I just felt it; that there would be trouble. Mac promised he would not go to the bar; promised not to drink. He kissed me and gave Mindy a peck on her forehead. He got in that white Oldsmobile and drove away. I never saw him alive again."

*****

Early Wednesday morning the telephone at Bert Porter's home rang. It rang again and Marilyn got out of bed. She glanced at the clock and noticing the time was a little after 2 a.m. she figured the bars had closed and Mac was calling. She answered the phone and said, "Hello."

A man's voice asked, "Is this Mrs. Griffith?"

"Yes," responded Marilyn warily.

"Your husband has been shot here in Prineville," said the impassive voice.

Marilyn's free hand came up to her mouth. She expelled a quick breath and asked, "Is he okay? How is he?"

The voice coldly stated, "Ma'am, he's dead."

A keening erupted from the pit of Marilyn's stomach. She dropped the phone, took an involuntary step backward, sank to her knees, bent at the waist, buried her face in her hands and sobbed uncontrollably. She remembers being overwhelmed by her emotions, saying, "I felt this crushing wave of sadness sweep over me. It drove me to the floor. I felt buried by that wave."

Bert did not try to console her daughter, but went directly to the phone. The receiver was swinging on the cord, bumping against the wall, and she picked it up and asked what had happened. The voice on the line explained there had been a fight in the parking lot behind the Ochoco Inn; Mac was dead from a gunshot wound to the stomach and an autopsy was scheduled for the morning. The voice asked where the body should be sent. Bert said, "Sweeney Mortuary in Heppner." After that conversation concluded, she made calls to Mac's mother, Eva, and to his brother, Don.

*****

"Odd as it might seem, I felt a need to see Mac one last time," said Marilyn. "After his body had been released, Mac's brother, Don, drove me to Heppner, to Sweeney Mortuary. Mr. Sweeney did everything he could to talk me out of viewing the body, saying Mac had been badly beaten and there was a lot of bruising; it would be better for me to remember him alive, rather than dead. I insisted, and finally Mr. Sweeney led me to the back room. Guaranteed, what I saw was a pretty stark and gruesome scene. Mac was in the middle of the room, lying on a metal gurney. A white sheet covered him from the waist down. I went over and stood beside him. I couldn't touch him, didn't want to touch him, and yet I wanted to touch him and kiss him, and tell him one more time I loved him. I did none of those things. I was in shock, I suppose. I just stood there; said nothing, did nothing.

"Mac had always seemed larger than life. I remembered him laughing and having a good time. My memories were of him riding, drinking and carrying on. He was this force of wild energy, and at rodeos everything spun around Mac Griffith. He was a bronc rider, bull rider, bulldogger and roper. And now in death he was nothing more than a lifeless shell of a man on a stainless steel gurney. It was so goddamn pitiful. I felt incredible anger that someone had taken his life.

"The body hardly resembled the Mac Griffith I had known and loved. Mr. Sweeney had tried to cover the many ugly black and blue bruises with heavy make-up, but there was no way to hide them. Mac had taken a terrible beating. Then I looked at Mac's hands and the knuckles were buggered up bad, and he even had a bandage wrapped around one finger. I thought, at least Mac got in a few good licks; had made the son of a bitch who killed him pay. That's what I thought. More than anything, I felt this incredible surge of sadness. Sadness Mac was gone from my life. Sadness Mindy would never know her father. I didn't even have a single tear to shed. I was all cried out."

*****

The service for Mac Griffith was held five days before Christmas, 1964, at the Heppner First Christian Church. The Reverend Bud Godby, known as the *Cowboy Preacher* and the official Rodeo Cowboys Association minister, from Gooding, Idaho, officiated. The obituary listed many of Mac's accomplishments and named those family members he left behind; wife, daughter, mother, five sisters and a brother. It stated, "Griffith was shot to death following an argument in Prineville," but gave no details of the event. Marilyn attended the service, and as the cowboys gathered and gave her their condolences, she listened as they spoke among themselves. She pieced together some of the story, learning Mac had gotten in a fistfight with an off-duty Oregon State policeman, Larry Irwin, and that Jim Bothum and Ronnie Raymond had tried to intercede and break up the fight. The shooter's name was Duane Harvey, a man from Prineville. According to the cowboys, Harvey had pulled his car around to where the fight was going on in the parking lot behind the Ochoco Inn, stepped out of his car armed with a derringer pistol and shot Mac at point black range. The bullet had nicked the aorta and Mac bled to death before they could get him to the hospital. Duane Harvey had been arrested and was being charged with murder one. The district attorney had him dead to rights. Harvey was going to the electric chair. That son of a bitch was going to get what he deserved. That was what the cowboys were saying.

Marilyn talked to Bud Godby before the service and he asked if she wanted him to say anything in particular. Marilyn said, "I asked him to mention this—it is man who looks on the outside, but it is God who looks on the inside—because deep down in his soul, Mac was a good man. God knew that. One time at the Tygh Valley Rodeo, I saw all these dirty, runny-nosed little Indian kids lined out behind Mac and he was leading them to the ice cream truck and buying each and every one of them an ice cream cone. Kids loved Mac, and he loved them back. Another thing about Mac, he never abused an animal. My dad beat horses with two-by-fours but not Mac. He respected animals.

"Most everyone saw Mac as one of the best rough stock riders in the world. They had this image of him as a man's man, bigger than life, with the potential to be the best cowboy of all time. I remember Mac barking, 'I'm a fucker, a fighter, a wild horse rider, and a mean son of a bitch when I'm drunk. And I'm drinking a little all the time.' And then he would give a whoop and leap into action, whether he was crawling on the back of a bronc, or a bull, or rolling up his sleeves to jump into a bar fight. In a nutshell that was the image Mac had of himself, and come hell or high water, he felt as though he had to live up to that image.

"Few people ever saw Mac's good side. He kept that hidden. In my opinion the real Mac Griffith was the man I married and spent that first winter with, back in the hills feeding cattle. As long as he rodeoed on weekends and worked during the week, he was fine. Then he only drank on weekends. He didn't go loop-legged until he joined the RCA. Professional cowboys live a different lifestyle. Mac's downfall was that lifestyle and his success, but more than anything it was the alcohol. Alcohol brought out the other Mac Griffith, or at least the dangerous side of his personality. If he could have left the booze alone, he would have been the World Champion All-Around cowboy and probably stayed there for 10 years or so before his body failed him. That's my opinion.

"The day of Mac's funeral was cold and miserable. The church overflowed with cowboys there to show their final respects. Sharon Bryant, Mac's girlfriend on the side, sat in the back row all teary eyed and emotional. During our marriage, she had been a real bone of contention between Mac and me. She was married, but never let that get in her way as she ran after Mac every damn chance she got. Seeing her there at his funeral irritated the hell out of me, but there was nothing I could do."

Mac was laid to rest in the Masonic Cemetery at Heppner. After his graveside service the cowboys gathered around a white-paper-covered table where a blue bucket of ice sat surrounded by jugs of red wine, half-gallons of Crown Royal, and a keg of beer. There were assorted cold cuts, cheeses, and crackers arranged in various circular patterns on two platters. The cowboys drank and ate, talked and smoked—the smell of cigarettes was as sharp as a knife blade—and after it was over, they scattered to the wind.

All that remained of Mac Griffith were stories of his wild escapades, a few belt buckles and trophy saddles he had won, and photographs of him riding, roping and bulldogging steers. There was no insurance money to be shared. According to the RCA insurance carrier, a cowboy was covered for 48 hours after leaving a rodeo, and since Mac died beyond that time period, he was not covered. All Marilyn received were two monthly checks from the Social Security Administration, one for her and one for Mindy, in the amount of $77.

Ralph Currin, the family's attorney from Pendleton, advised Marilyn she had a strong case if she wanted to sue the Cinnabar Lounge and the Ochoco Inn. He claimed the autopsy revealed Mac had a blood alcohol level of .23 percent, and the establishment that had served him was responsible for his intoxication and was legally liable. Marilyn said she was not interested in suing anyone, and that was the end of it.

*****

At the trial for Duane Harvey, the man accused of murdering Mac Griffith, the defense employed a very unusual legal maneuver to keep Marilyn from the courtroom. Marilyn was subpoenaed by the defense, but was never called to testify. The defense, fearing the widow might evoke a twinge of sympathy for the victim in the minds of the jury, especially if she brought along her child, kept Marilyn from setting foot in the courtroom. The prosecutor, Doug Shepard, never objected to this tactic by the defense, even though he could have argued Marilyn was not a material witness, and therefore could offer no testimony about the killing.

"Once the trial started they kept me and the other witnesses in a room adjacent to the main courtroom," said Marilyn. "I could hear some of what was going on and if I stood on my tip-toes, I could peek through a small window. From what I was able to hear and see, I would definitely say the deck was stacked against a fair trial. It was a blatant character assassination against Mac. The defense had dug up every bad thing Mac had ever done and used it all against him. Mac was made out to be this horrible person lacking even a single shred of decency. The prosecution never objected. That was just not right.

"The trial lasted a week and every day the courtroom was jam packed with people lined up in the hallway and down the stairs. The defense attorney, Mr. Bodie, put on quite a show.

He was a skilled orator and his performance was worthy of an Oscar nomination. He was that good.

"During the summation, I peeked through the window and Mr. Bodie was crying like a baby, wiping at his tears with his white hankie and blowing his nose loudly. I thought he must have an onion hidden in his handkerchief because he could produce tears like turning a faucet. Finally he threw up his hands and left the courtroom in a huff. His assistant, Jim Minturn, finished up with some cock-and-bull story about a woman who got murdered in New York City. What did that have to do with Mac getting shot? Absolutely nothing.

"The jury didn't take long to deliberate. I was standing in the hallway when they came back with their verdict. Someone from the Harvey family laughed and said that was a good sign for acquittal. I scowled at him.

"After the verdict was read, Mr. Bodie made a point of coming over to me and apologizing for keeping me from the courtroom. I told him, 'Mr. Bodie, if I ever kill somebody, I know the man I'm going to get to defend me and that's you.' He never acknowledged what I said, just turned and walked away.

"Mac's car, the Oldsmobile, was released to me since my name was on the title. It had a lot of miles on it, but it was paid for and I drove that car for several months; then traded it for a pea-green Chevy Biscayne, a plain-Jane with a stick shift and no radio. The Olds had too many memories. I didn't want it anymore.

"Not long after the trial, an Indian girl from Chiloquin got in touch with me. She said Mac hocked one of his trophy saddles to her to raise his money for his entry fees at the Klamath Falls rodeo. She wanted me to have the saddle. I thanked her and took it.

"When times got really tough for Mindy and me, I sold the saddle and the bronze C. A. Biel trophies that Mac won at the Calgary Stampede; one for bulldogging and one for saddle bronc. They were beautiful, but you can't eat beauty. I got $1,200 for one and $2,200 for the other. Recently one of those bronzes came up for auction and sold for more than $50,000.

Had I hung onto the trophies I would have lost them because in 1975 my house burned to the ground and nothing was saved.

"For the most part, I'm one to let bygones be bygones, but one day I got a wild hair—must have been 20 or 25 years after the shooting—and called Duane Harvey. I told him who I was and said there were a few things I would kinda like to know. Dead silence. He refused to say anything. I asked him if he would be willing to talk to me. He hung up the phone. If I could have talked to Duane Harvey, I'd have asked him what led up to the fight, what his ex-wife and the barmaid had to do with things, and why, since he wasn't involved in the fight, didn't he just walk away, rather than pull out a gun and shoot a defenseless man? He never gave me the satisfaction of answering those questions.

"The hardest part for me to have lived with all these years is that, just before he died, Mac had wanted to change his ways, be a good husband and a good father. But he didn't know how to change. He was clueless. He had constructed this image of himself and was powerless to step away from it. But I think he was coming to a point in his life where he knew the fame and glory weren't going to last forever. He wasn't invincible and he knew that, too.

"I think in today's world, a doctor would examine Mac and diagnose him as being bipolar. He showed all the classic symptoms. The hard knocks, his alcohol consumption and the lifestyle he led, all worked against him. Mindy followed in Mac's footsteps to some degree. Doctors made the diagnosis that she is bipolar, an aggressive type that has limited her ability to function as an adult. They say a parent passes on those genes to their children. I don't have it. It had to come from somewhere.

"One time Mindy told me she really didn't think about her daddy all that much, but based on what she knew about him, she didn't think she would have liked him. That just about broke my heart; that she was never allowed the opportunity to get to know her father."

Mac Griffith & Margaret "Sharon" Bryant,
Heppner High School Yearbook, 1956

The Girlfriend

Margaret "Sharon" Bryant was the product of a broken home. Her mother divorced her alcoholic husband in the sawmill town of Potlatch, Idaho and shipped Sharon to Heppner, Oregon, to live with her 80-year-old grandmother. For the first eight years of her schooling, Sharon had attended a private Catholic school for girls, but to start high school, she enrolled in the public school in Heppner. Her classmates described Sharon as very naïve and a *wallflower,* who was easily embarrassed and quick to blush.

In Sharon's sophomore year, the Griffith family moved from Redmond, Oregon, to Heppner, and Sharon found herself immediately drawn to Mac Griffith. And why shouldn't she be drawn to him? He was popular, self-confident, good-looking, outgoing, boisterous, a natural athlete and he was always the center of attention. He was the class clown, a talker and a troublemaker. He was everything Sharon was not.

The sophomore class had study hall in a room adjacent to the principal's office. There was a window in the common wall, painted over except for a small circle. Whenever the principal, Mr. Dobbie, wanted to check on students and make sure they were behaving, he peered through that peephole. If someone in the room was talking or causing a disturbance, he rapped his knuckles on the glass, pointed to the offender and motioned for that individual to come to his office. Mac, with his proclivity for talking and pulling juvenile stunts, was a regular visitor to the principal's office.

One night someone slipped inside the school and painted over the circle. When Mr. Dobbie confronted Mac about his possible involvement, Mac screwed his expression into shocked disbelief and defensively exclaimed, "You think I'm the type of person who would plan out something so elaborate? Place a book of matches between the fire escape door and the jam, and come up those rickety stairs carrying a bucket of paint and a brush in the dead of night? How could you even think such a thing of me?" Mac went unpunished, even though he purposely left the book of matches and a smear of paint on the fire escape.

Mac had a competitive side to his personality and constantly tested the boundaries to see what he could get away with. One morning the FFA display in the school's glass trophy case had a new addition, a photograph of a hog reclining in the mud with a typed caption reading, "Mr. Dobbie, relaxing at home." Again Mac Griffith was suspected, but Mr. Dobbie was the only person with a key and how Mac could have managed to open the locked trophy case was never solved, and the culprit went unpunished. This incident only enhanced Mac's growing reputation as a prankster.

Mac did get in trouble when, in a crowded hallway between classes, he affixed a sign on the back of one of the teachers which read, "Kick My Butt." In class, and unaware of the sign, the teacher stepped to the chalkboard and the students erupted in laughter. Mac was immediately sent to the principal's office. Sharon found him there, sitting with a pair of baseball shoes on his lap, head hanging low in mock shame. He mournfully said, "My poor widowed mother had to break her piggy bank to buy me these cleats, and now I get myself in trouble and they won't even let me suit up for the big ball game. This will break my momma's heart."

Sharon thought Mac was funny, and in turn he took great delight in making her laugh. Before long, Mac was walking Sharon home from school, even though he lived on the opposite side of town. The unlikely friendship between the two continued to grow, and Sharon even learned to crawl out of her protective shell and pull a practical joke on fun-loving Mac.

The study hall before lunch was supervised by a timid teacher, and the boys took advantage of her, having her sign hall passes to go to the bathroom and then slipping out of school to go downtown to the pool hall. Sharon got her best friend, Judy Wright, to make a call to the pool hall. Judy left a message for Mac, saying she was the school secretary and ordering him to immediately report to Mr. Dobbie's office. When Mac walked into the office he addressed Mr. Dobbie, asking, "You wanted to see me?"

"I don't know what you're talking about. I never sent for you," said Mr. Dobbie. And Mac knew he had been set up. It took him a long time before he figured out the culprits were Judy and Sharon.

"Mac was a hoot," said Judy. "But you never wanted to dare him to do something, because no matter what it was, he took the dare. He was wild like that."

Sharon was a good student while Mac rarely applied himself to school work. He was content to slide through his studies with grades barely passable, but good enough to allow him to participate in sports. To make sure Mac got his homework completed on time, Sharon helped him. In class she sat beside him and allowed him to see her test answers. On one test Sharon was in a hurry and made a mistake. Mac copied her mistake and passed on his answers to his friends. After the teacher graded the tests she announced, "We have a problem.

Nearly all of you answered one of the questions with the same wrong answer."

Mac leaped to his feet and proclaimed, "Ma'am, I'm very concerned about this situation. I'm just afraid everyone might have copied my test." His statement brought a boisterous hoot of laughter from the students because nobody would ever want to copy Mac's answers on a test. The teacher never pursued the matter, and the possibility of cheating was simply dropped.

Mac was known for being a tough, athletic kid. He was the starting halfback and linebacker on the high school football team. He played baseball and was an all-star pitcher and a hitter with sufficient power to hit a home run every time he stepped to the plate. But his combination of amazing balance, brute strength and grit was best suited for the sport of rodeo. He consistently won the rough stock riding events and was the Junior Rodeo All-Around Champion.

Sharon and Judy discovered that Mac, to earn money for his entry fees at the rodeos, was babysitting one of the teacher's two young daughters. They teased him and Mac gave them a hard, serious look, said, "Don't you say nothin' about this to nobody; not a word. If something like this gets out it'll destroy my reputation. Keep it to yourselves, or I'll have to kill you." He smiled, but there had been a rigid edge to the way he spoke that let Sharon and Judy know Mac was not joking. He did not want anyone to expose what might possibly be construed as his *soft* side.

In his senior year, Mac was a trendsetter. Singer Pat Boone came out with his number one Billboard hit, *Kid in the White Buck Shoes,* and it was Mac who was the first at Heppner High School to own and wear a pair of white buck shoes. Nobody teased him because nobody ever dared to tease Mac Griffith, not unless that person wanted to end up in a fistfight. Sharon said, "He was protective of those shoes; made sure they never had a scuff mark and polished them every night."

Mac did not have a car. His mother, Eva, did not have a car. When Mac asked Sharon on dates, they usually walked uptown for a bite to eat, or to the show house to catch the latest movie.

Their relationship progressed from friends, to best friends, and finally to lovers. Sharon said, "It was a gradual thing. It just happened. We didn't have many opportunities as lovers, but we made the most of the times we had. And I was so dumb about that sort of thing. I just trusted I wouldn't get pregnant. Thankfully, I never did. But really, what Mac and I had, had very little to do with the act of sex. We shared a love affair. And we did love each other. We had an intense intimacy. The sex part was just the frosting on the cake."

Sharon was the editor of the *Mustang,* the Heppner High School Yearbook, for 1956. She did the layout for senior photographs and positioned her photograph and Mac's photograph on facing pages, so that forever after they would be together. At that point, Sharon really did believe they would get married, have a family together and live happily ever after. But as their senior year wound down to the last few weeks, Sharon's plans and dreams were turned upside down the night a group of seniors went out to drink beer and have fun. Mac had borrowed a pickup truck and at the end of the night, he dropped off kids at their respective homes. It was down to just two passengers, Sharon and a girl named Christine. Mac dropped Sharon off first, and she thought nothing of Mac being alone with Christine. But the following day at school, Christine had her right arm in a cast and sling and the rumor circulated she had broken her arm trying to fight off the advances of Mac Griffith and that he had forced her to have sex. Sharon was humiliated. She believed the outrage was true, and as the last few days of school passed, she never spoke to Mac and refused to even look in his direction. Then school was over and Mac was gone, chasing Northwest Rodeo Association (NRA) rodeos around the Northwest. His star was on the rise, and he rarely came home to Heppner.

That summer a local farmer, Kenny Cutsforth, made a play for Sharon. He asked her on dates, and at first she refused to go out with him, but Kenny was persistent. He bought expensive gifts, showered her with attention and affection, and eventually Sharon did go on a date with him. What she secretly hoped for was that Mac would hear she was seeing someone, come home and profess his undying love for her. Then she and Mac would marry and life would be wonderful. But Mac never did call Sharon.

Months passed and Sharon and Kenny became lovers. According to Sharon, the first time she and Kenny had sex, she got pregnant. Kenny insisted they get married, and Sharon didn't know what else to do. She married Kenny and he moved her out of town to his ranch at Sand Hollow. After the baby was born, he informed her that his plan was to keep her barefoot and pregnant. He did a good job of it, and Sharon had three children in quick succession. Even though, according to Sharon, the marriage was a dismal failure from the start, she did what was expected of her. She cooked, kept house and raised the children. Sharon said, "I was forced to accept Kenny's verbal and physical abuse, and to endure his frequent affairs. I played the devoted wife until the spring of 1963 when Mac Griffith called me out of the blue. He said he was in town, and asked me to meet him at his mother's house. He said he would be alone and that he needed to talk to me."

Sharon had never stopped loving Mac, and had followed his meteoric career as he rose through the ranks of amateur and then professional rodeo. She readily agreed to meet him, but knowing the risk of exposing her true feelings, she took her baby along to ensure she would not fall into Mac's willing arms and do something stupid. She sat on the couch in Eva's living room, holding her baby on her lap, and listened as Mac talked, pouring out his heart to her. He said he married Marilyn to get back at Sharon for marrying Kenny. He claimed his marriage was doomed, and confessed that women were constantly throwing themselves at him. He admitted he took these women to bed at every opportunity, and then he told Sharon, "All those women are nothing but *civilians* to me. They're not my friends, will never be my friends. I love 'em and I leave 'em. They help me pass the time. They're not like you. You're not a *civilian*. I love you."

Sharon was sitting opposite from where Mac was seated in a straight-back chair. He got up and moved to sit beside her on the couch. He slung a brawny arm around her shoulders and hugged her. The baby squirmed, wanting to be put down, and Sharon placed him on a blanket on the floor. It was then that Mac took Sharon's face in his big, rough hands, turned her head upward and forced her to look at him. But Sharon was not willing to give in—not yet. She said, "What about Christine?"

Mac laughed, said she hurt her arm while they were wrestling, and it was all very playful and totally innocent. He claimed nothing sexual had happened. Sharon wanted to believe him. Then Mac kissed her, kissed her hard on the lips and all the feelings she had for him, and managed to keep hidden for seven long years, burst forth into a gusher of emotions. She sobbed and Mac kissed away her tears. He told her he loved her, that he had never stopped loving her and would love her forever.

Sharon, living with a husband who only criticized her and never offered a compliment or showed any semblance of affection, was susceptible to the words Mac spoke, and the ardor with which he delivered those words. She urgently needed to be loved. When she return Mac's kiss, it was with more passion than she thought she could possibly possess. Again she cried, and after that she sat beside Mac, hips touching, kissing occasionally, but mainly just talking, until the sun dipped below the shoulder of the hill. When Sharon realized the time, and knowing she was expected to have dinner on the table for Kenny, she leaped to her feet, scooped her son off the floor and announced she had to go.

That evening, as Sharon served dinner, Kenny demanded to know where she had been and what she had been doing. She told the truth, a slim portion of the truth, admitted to visiting Eva Griffith, even though she had not been home. Kenny smirked, said, "Yeah, I heard Mac was in town." Then he asked, "You see him?"

"Just in passing," fibbed Sharon. "He came in as I was leaving."

*****

"After our talk at Eva's house," said Sharon, "Mac began calling my home in the middle of the night, after the bars closed. He was always very considerate, and asked if I was free to talk. If Kenny was awake, I'd say, 'I'm sorry, but you have the wrong number.' As I was hanging up the phone, Mac would apologize, saying something sweet like he just called because he needed to hear my voice, or that he loved me. If Kenny was asleep or gone, Mac and I talked for hours."

"Mac was a big time rodeo star," said Judy Wright. "When he couldn't talk to Sharon, he called me. It was pretty obvious that I became their go-between. Mac invited us to rodeos, and if Sharon could figure out a good excuse for going, we'd hop in the car and go. Sharon made a real point of saying she and Mac had a *special friendship*. She never wanted to face the truth, that what she and Mac were having was an *affair*. They went to bed together, sure, but it was way more than just a physical relationship. Those two shared an incredible love. They were still like a couple of high school teenagers, laughing and giggling and talking and hugging. They were perfectly suited, but they were both married, and not to each other. That was a problem, a big problem, especially in a small town like Heppner."

*****

Mac never tried to hide the fact he had many women in his life. He told Sharon about the women he took to bed, and the professional girls he visited in Nevada. He said one of his frequent haunts was the *Circle* in Winnemucca. He described the *Circle* as a group of whorehouses off an alleyway, and said that whenever he was broke, he went there to hock one of his trophy saddles; usually he ended up with a girl for the night and enough money in his pocket for his entry fees at the next rodeo.

Sharon and Judy got a firsthand look at Mac with one of his lady friends after attending the Round-Up. They went to the Hut to grab a bite to eat before heading home and Mac came out of the bar into the restaurant, saw them and sat at their table. Before long a leggy brunette emerged from the bar and tried to cajole Mac away. He was curt with her; said he would see her later and that he was busy talking to friends.

"Best not let her get away," kidded Sharon.

"There's a hundred more where she came from," said Mac. "I can have any of those *buckle bunnies* whenever I want, but I don't have the time to spend with my real friends, not very often, and so I want to make the most of this opportunity." He hugged Sharon and she felt as though, in Mac's eyes, she was the only woman in the world. When the brunette reappeared, and stood impatiently beside the table, Mac pulled his wallet from his hind pocket, removed a five-dollar bill and gave it to the girl along with the rebuke, "Catch a cab, sweetheart. I'm busy."

He turned to Sharon and said, "I'd rather have a few minutes with you than all night with whatever she has to offer."

*****

Mac invited Sharon and Judy to the 1963 rodeo in Las Vegas. Initially the idea of accepting the invitation seemed out of the question. It was too far, would cost too much, and anyway, their husbands would never allow them to run off to Las Vegas and leave their children behind. But Sharon was adamant about going, and she devised a plan to surprise Mac and just show up at the rodeo. She found a motel in Las Vegas accepting S & H Green Stamps—16 books of stamps per night—and if she and Judy pooled their books, they had enough to cover the cost of three nights lodging at the motel.

Sharon screwed up her courage and talked to Kenny, proposing a girls' trip to Las Vegas, but of course, she never bothered to mention the rodeo or her plans to surprise Mac. She reasoned it would cost next to nothing, a few books of

Green Stamps to pay for the room and breakfast was included. They would play nickel slots and maybe catch a show or two. It would all be harmless fun. Kenny grumbled, "If you go runnin' off, who's gonna watch the kids?"

"You are," said Sharon boldly. "You and your buddies get away to go deer hunting, elk hunting, bird hunting, fishing, and I'm left to guard the fort. Fair play is fair play. Judy and I need a little R & R, just like you men get to enjoy."

After several days of pressure, Kenny reluctantly gave in. On a sunny Friday morning, at 5 a.m., Sharon and Judy gleefully tossed suitcases in the trunk of the Cutsforth's brand new Ford Galaxie 500—a bright red 2-door hardtop, white leather interior, 352 V8, Cruise-O-Matic—and they roared out of Heppner, headed as due south as the country roads allowed, driving fast, pushing the speedometer over 100 miles per hour on the straight-aways, stopping only when they needed gas and a potty break. They passed the Las Vegas city limit sign at 7 p.m. and after checking into their motel—paying with 48 books of S & H Green Stamps—they made a mad dash for the rodeo. When they found Mac, he was shocked to see them, but recovered quickly, and after the rodeo they went out for a night on the town.

Mac told Sharon and Judy that he was sharing a room with his traveling partner, Marty Wood, at the Thunderbird Hotel. But when he took Sharon to the room they found it empty. They caught up to Marty in the bar. He claimed the hotel management had taken objection to his antics at the pool with an airline stewardess and had tossed him out of the hotel. Mac shrugged and lied to Sharon, saying he only had the clothes on his back and no place to stay. He failed to mention his belongings, as well as his pregnant wife, Marilyn, were in his room at another hotel. Sharon suggested Mac stay in their room, but Mac declined, saying he did not want to get them in trouble. "We're in party town, USA," laughed Mac. "Night and day are the same. Let's party!"

The girls from Heppner were tucked inside the tight circle of professional rodeo cowboys as they swept along the lively

Las Vegas strip; drinking, gambling and pulling good-natured practical jokes. Ronnie Raymond got hold of a hand truck and made a spectacle of dashing about the casino floor, scooping up unwitting victims, tilting them backward and spinning them around the room. It took several security guards to overpower the wiry cowboy, and once he was restrained, they wheeled him outside on the hand truck and unceremoniously dumped him on the sidewalk. What did it matter? All the cowboys, with Sharon and Judy in tow, were off to the next casino. Everyone was having fun.

"Judy and I were dumber than posts, real hicks from the sticks," said Sharon. "I was sitting alone at a table with four chairs. Mac was off with his buddies and Judy was playing the nickel slots. A guy came over and asked if I'd mind if he helped himself to a chair. I said sure, that there were only three of us. I had no idea the guy was trying to pick me up. He plopped down in the chair beside me and called to the bartender to bring us drinks. I was scared to death. If Mac had come back, he would've kicked the guy's ass. I told the man he better get out of there because my date was a professional fighter. He took the hint and skedaddled."

The group partied away the night, and they partied the next day until it was time for the rodeo. When the final event ended, the party picked up where it had left off. Nobody slept, and with alcohol as their fuel, they kept the throttle wide open.

On the last day of the rodeo, after the bull riding ended, Mac announced, "When the show is over, I collect my winnings and get the hell out of Dodge. If you stick around this town, it'll bleed you dry and you'll end up dead broke, lying in a ditch somewhere on the other side of the city limit sign." He went on to claim he and his traveling partner, Marty Wood, were off to chase the next rodeo. But when Mac left Sharon and Judy, he did not go with Marty Wood, but actually doubled back to where Marilyn, his pregnant wife, was holed up in the hotel room. For the past three days and nights she had been too sick to leave the room. And Mac had not a single excuse to offer for his absence.

Sharon and Judy left Las Vegas. They allowed the big V8 to growl away the miles as they headed north; windows down, radio blaring, trading off driving, the passenger catching up on much needed sleep.

*****

"It was a different era back in the early '60s," said Judy. "Those were the days when cowboys rode hard and played harder. Sure they drank too much and got in fistfights, but when the fights were over, they bought each other drinks and were still friends. We had fun with that bunch of cowboys in Las Vegas, and we had the pleasure of their company in a lot of other rodeo towns, too.

"My favorite rodeo was the PI (Pacific International Livestock Exposition) in Portland. My parents lived in the Willamette Valley and they provided a good excuse for Sharon and me to get away for a few days. We spent most of our time at the Red Barn, a bar near the rodeo grounds.

"One time Mac had to drive one of his friends across the river to Vancouver, Washington. We all went along for the ride, and as we approached the toll bridge, Mac asked if anyone had change for the toll. Sharon and I were frantically searching our purses for change when Mac bellowed, 'Ah, hell, forget it.' He stomped on the accelerator and wheeled through the toll booth. Red lights flashed, but we never slowed. On the return trip, Mac did the same thing. That was just Mac being Mac. He was always wild and borderline out of control. He lived life like he rode rough stock, taking chances, spurring all the way and very seldom suffering consequences for his actions. And usually, Mac had a crowd following in his wake."

*****

A few months before his death, Mac invited Sharon and Judy to the Lewiston rodeo. Sharon said, "Judy and I drove to Lewiston—our excuse was to visit my sister in Idaho—and we went to the hotel where Mac was staying. The clerk at the lobby desk rang his room, but it was not Mac who answered the phone. It was some cowboy I didn't know. I asked if Mac was there. He said he wasn't, but gave me another room to call. When I did talk to Mac, I asked what was going on with all the cloak-and-dagger. He explained he never stayed in his room, that he always traded rooms. He said, 'I don't wanna get shot,' and went on to say, 'I've been on the road a lot of years now, and I've slept with guys' girlfriends and wives. If one of those men gets liquored up, he might wanna come after me.'

"That night Mac and I were alone. He told me he was trying to slow down, that his traveling partner, Marty Wood, was a good influence. Marty had said if Mac were to concentrate on rodeo, he could be the World All-Around Champion. Mac talked about the pressure he felt having to uphold the image he had created; the tough guy, the lover, the All-Around cowboy. He said it was wearing thin, having to be all those things. He no longer wanted to go to bars and have to fight. But he did. He didn't want to take every pretty girl to bed, but he certainly did. He said he felt trapped on his own merry-go-round and couldn't step off. That was how he put it.

"Then, when Mac told me about a reccurring dream he was having, he actually got tears in his eyes. In the dream a man—he never saw the man's face—pulled out a gun and shot Mac in the stomach. Mac said he could hear the wallop of the slug hitting him, and could feel the pain; like a red-hot poker shoved into him. Then he became real serious and said, 'I'll get shot and die before I'm 30.' He was resigned to getting shot and there was nothing I could say, or do, to reassure him it was only a dream. He was adamant he was going to die before he was 30.

"While we were in Lewiston, I never went to bed with Mac. We just talked, and talked, and talked some more. He told me he loved me and asked if I still loved him. I said, 'I wouldn't be here with you now if I didn't love you. Of course I love you.' He said his relationship with Marilyn was over, and regretted his little girl, Mindy, was now part of his and Marilyn's mess.

He wanted to marry me, but he said the road wasn't a good place for me, and he wouldn't think about dragging me from one hotel to the next, especially not with my three kids. He really did want us to be together, but he was realistic.

"Mac was planning to make a big swing and hit rodeos in New York, Boston, Toronto and Chicago. He was hoping to do well and move up in the All-Around standings. His goal was to be number one in the world. After the season ended, he promised we would get together, talk about our situation and maybe he would bunch the circuit and we could buy a ranch somewhere in Eastern Oregon and settle down together as a family. I think he knew if he didn't step away from the professional circuit, it was going to kill him. And I think he really did love me. The last thing he said before we parted was, 'Someday we're gonna have a life together. You just gotta believe ... someday.' He wrapped his arms around me, held me tightly in his embrace and kissed me. It was the last time I saw him alive."

*****

Sharon's grandmother called with the disturbing news Mac Griffith had been shot during an argument in a Prineville bar. The call was not totally unexpected. Sharon realized Mac lived on the ragged edge of a dangerous life. Her first thought was to recall Mac's dream—the faceless man with the gun—and she asked, "What hospital is he in, Prineville or Bend?"

Phone static hissed in Sharon's ear, a long moment passed and then her grandmother said, "He's not in any hospital. Honey, he's dead."

A strange silence rushed in like feathers falling, drifting downward, and Sharon's body tilted toward an unsupported fall. She caught herself and plopped onto a kitchen chair, her mind teeming and whirling with remembrances of Mac coming at her as silver reflections advancing and retreating, enlarging and diminishing in a ghostly mosaic of flickering images. Her lips trembled. Bitterness, injustice, loss, anguish, sorrow and misery lodged in her throat as a dense lump. A harsh bleating of pain rose from her solar plexus, squeezed up her dusty throat and poured forth in a gurgle of sound. Scalding tears spilled in a downpour that could not be restricted, slowed, or stopped.

*****

"Sharon called me right away," said Judy Wright. "She was hysterical. I went right over, found her lying on the bed, arms wrapped tightly around her knees, body quaking, teeth chattering. Every few seconds long shivers swept through her, making her muscles twitch and jump. There really wasn't much I could do except cover her with a blanket, and try to comfort her. It was a very difficult time; I was trying to deal with my own grief, too.

"I fixed tea and helped Sharon drink some. I told her she had her children to think about, and for their sake she needed to pull herself out of her tailspin. She eventually was able to at least function well enough to cook and take care of her kids."

*****

Sharon insisted on attending the funeral, held the Saturday before Christmas at the Heppner First Christian Church. She thought she owed it to Mac to be there. Sharon and Judy sat on chairs in the back of the room. The lone memory Sharon has of that bitterly cold and snowy day was the puddles of water she observed around peoples' feet. She was not capable of comprehending snow melting off boots in the warm church. In Sharon's distorted perception and grief she thought this was the saddest funeral she had ever attended, that people were crying and their tears were pooling at their feet.

*****

Mac's death, and the finality of his funeral, caused Sharon to suffer under the strain of a deep emotional upheaval, and at odd and unexpected times she found the shine of sad tears on her cheeks. Nobody seemed to understand the depth of her grief and despair, not even her best friend, Judy; especially not her husband, Kenny. His solution was for Sharon to "just get over it." He was exasperated with her and once, thinking he was being sympathetic and supportive, made the insensitive remark, "All through our marriage, Mac Griffith was a constant thorn in my side. Now that he's gone, it'll all be better." Taken at face value, Kenny's remark was a fact as he perceived it, but to Sharon his words were like the grating ends of a broken bone. And now, when he came in from the fields, just the sight of him sickened her. She refused his touch, and began dressing and undressing in the bathroom and sleeping curled under a blanket on the couch.

"One morning I just up and jumped into the fire. I filed for divorce," said Sharon. "After that, there was no turning back. But you know I never regretted my marriage to Kenny. I have three wonderful children. It just came to the point I couldn't live with that man anymore.

"In all the years that have passed since Mac died, it has never gotten any easier for me to accept the fact he is gone. If he had lived, he would be an old man now, probably bald and cantankerous as all get out. It makes me laugh to think of him that way. Mac and I could have made a pretty good life together, if we had had the chance. I know I will always hold a special place for him in my heart."

Marty Wood, 2014

The Traveling Partner

Marty Wood, a Canadian cowboy from the province of Alberta, was born in 1933. His father owned and operated Wood's Riding Academy. That was where Marty learned to ride, break and show horses. But he turned away from the discipline of showing horses and gravitated to the sport of rodeo. He won his first professional saddle bronc riding event in Omaha, Nebraska, in 1953. During his two-decade long rodeo career, Marty won the saddle bronc championship at the Calgary Stampede a total of five times, and won at Cheyenne, Madison Square Garden, San Francisco Cow Palace, Fort Worth, Houston, Salinas, Boston Garden and Oklahoma City. He was the three-time Canadian Saddle Bronc Champion and three-time World Saddle Bronc Champion.

When Marty was at his best, one of his main traveling partners was Mac Griffith. Nobody in their right mind would have put the two men together. Marty was short and built slight and wiry. He was always well groomed, had good manners and was intelligent and well-spoken. He was a married man and he and Ruth Ann had one child, a son, Chip. Connecting Marty and Mac was their mutual love for the sport of rodeo, comparable riding abilities, fierce competitiveness and an unbridled passion for milking every ounce of excitement and joy from each day, and night.

"First time I ran across Mac Griffith was at the Pendleton Round-Up," said Marty. "What impressed me was the way this big, rawboned kid could compete in so many events. He rode saddle bronc, bareback and bulls. He bulldogged and roped steers too. He was an all-around hand, good at everything and capable of winning any event he entered. Usually a cowboy favors one event, maybe two, but Mac was rock solid at everything he did. His versatility was astounding. He had God-given natural ability, sure, but it was evident he had spent a lot of effort honing his skills. I thought to myself, 'This kid has what it takes to be the World All-Around Cowboy.'"

In an effort to make as many rodeos as possible, Marty bought a new, decked out 1958 Chevrolet Impala. Over the next year he drove to nearly 100 rodeos and put over a hundred thousand miles on the flashy car. He bought a new car every year, going from the Impala, to a Thunderbird, to a Chrysler 300, and then settling on Oldsmobile; an 88, and after that buying nothing but 98s.

"As I went down the road I'd keep crossing paths with Mac Griffith," said Marty, "The kid was getting better every time he competed, but outside rodeo he had a reputation for being a tad on the wild side. Hell, I liked to have a good time too, and after a rodeo, if I wasn't headed somewhere, I'd go to my hotel room, get cleaned up and enjoy a night on the town. I believe a fellow needs to take his fun where he finds it.

"Mac and I, we tipped a few. He was a good guy to bullshit with and we got along fine. But you sure as hell didn't want to get on Mac's bad side. If he liked you, he told you so. And if he didn't, you knew that, too. That's just the way it was with Mac. He laid all the cards on the table, face up."

Mac idolized Marty Wood for his success riding saddle broncs, and for his free-wheeling lifestyle. In the rough and tumble world of rodeo, where a cowboy was constantly getting dirty and scuffed, Marty was an anomaly. He always looked clean and respectable. Marty explained, "It was easy for me to keep clean. I rode one event and my day was done. Most cowboys bought western shirts with snap buttons. I never liked snaps, and besides, a button-up white shirt was half the price of a western shirt. I'd have a stack of white shirts, and after using a shirt and getting it dirty, I threw it away. People thought I was a snappy dresser, but really I was just getting by on the cheap. Mac caught on to what I was doing and started wearing white shirts too. But working all those events, a single shirt usually never lasted Mac through an entire rodeo.

"I really don't know when Mac and I started partnering up. It was something that just happened. The first I remember us traveling together was after the Round-Up—must have been along about 1961—I was headed out to the next rodeo, which was Omaha—Mac crawled in my car and sat down. We traded off driving, made the rodeo, both got paydays, and after that we went down the road together. At first we took my car, but Mac bought a white Olds 98 and sometimes we drove his rig. It was pretty much a catch-as-catch-can and on down the highway you go."

Marty claims he never saw Mac go out of his way to start a fight, but if a fight broke out, Mac was always firmly planted in the middle of it. Marty said, "Some cowboys shied away from fights, but Mac could always be counted on to back up his friends. I've seen fights where it looked like a scene from a Western movie with bar stools and chairs flying, bottles breaking, cowboys standing toe-to-toe trading punches, and Mac would usually be the last man standing.

"When I first got to know Mac, he was pretty rowdy and had the attitude he could ride the toughest bronc or bull, whip the toughest son of a bitch in the bar, and was entitled to take the prettiest gal in town to bed. But I spent a lot of time with Mac, and told him point blank, if he continued down the road he was headed, he was gonna get the boot from the RCA. If that happened, he was out of professional rodeo and he'd be working for day wages on some two-bit ranch out of Monument or Condon. A man just can't burn the candle on both ends and expect the candle to last. Mac did listen to me, took my advice to heart, and gradually his personality started to change. He became more calm and relaxed, more focused on rodeo. I told Mac the only thing that could ever stop Mac Griffith from being the World All-Around Champion was Mac Griffith. If he focused on rodeo, he was a solid lock.

"When Mac drank his personality changed, but hell, everybody's personality changes with alcohol. What's that bar sign say? Something like, 'Alcohol makes you think you're better looking, tougher and more intelligent than you actually are,' and there's some truth to that saying. But hand it to Mac, drinking or not, he did enjoy life. He was a damn good friend to me and to a lot of other rodeo cowboys, too.

"Mac enjoyed shooting shuffleboard and playing the mini bowling machine they had in bars back in the '60s. He wasn't much of a card player because he wasn't very good at gambling. But he played a little pitch now and then like most of the cowboys did.

"Mac could hold his alcohol like few other men ever could. He never got falling-down drunk. He reached a certain level of intoxication and maintained that level; never getting sloppy. And when he was drinking, *especially* when he was drinking, Mac refused to take an ounce of shit off anyone. If a man mouthed off, Mac wasn't averse to telling him to shut the hell up. Mac was willing to fight at the drop of a hat, and if the man was bigger than Mac, so much the better in Mac's book. He enjoyed the challenge of going up against the best.

"I was in San Jose when I got the news Mac had been shot and killed at the Cinnabar Lounge in Prineville. I had been in that particular bar lots of times. It was a shotgun affair, a long narrow room with subdued lighting; a place where cowboys, loggers and mill workers stood elbow to elbow and belly to the bar. Prineville was a tough town. Someone told me, the year before Mac got killed, there was some ungodly number of killings in Crook County and not a single person ever went to the penitentiary. The word was, if you wanted to kill somebody and get away with it, you took 'em to Crook County to pull the trigger.

"As far as what happened the night Mac died, what I was told, was Mac and Ronnie Raymond were messing with a local fellow's ex-wife. An off-duty state cop got involved. Someone pulled a pistol. Mac got gut shot—a senseless thing—and the trial was a farce. The defense made Mac out to be a bully, a professional boxer who went around beating up people for the fun of it. The jury based their verdict on the misguided notion that Mac was such a bad egg that the local fellow was justified in killing him. Why didn't the prosecution counter that bullshit and show what Mac was really like? Why wasn't I called as a character witness? I would have testified in Mac's behalf and told it the way it was; Mac was a good guy, a good friend and he didn't deserve to die like that.

"I respected Mac as a cowboy, and I respected him as a man. You never had to worry about your back when you were with Mac. He had only begun to scratch the surface of his true potential. He was getting his life together, was coming around and would have made it if he hadn't got killed and died young.

"Hell, if Mac was alive, I'd buy that big bugger a drink. We'd sit around and talk about the old days, and how he had won the World All-Around 10 years running."

Pendleton Round-Up, 2013

Friends & Enemies

The consensus of opinion from the men who competed against Mac Griffith was the Eastern Oregon cowboy had incredible talents in the rodeo arena. They knew him to be a young man with courage, confidence and a firm belief in the Darwinian principle of survival of the fittest. In Mac's world, there was no room for weaklings. While he could be sensitive and caring, especially with animals and children, there was also a coarse, volatile and brutal side to Mac's personality that came to the forefront when he was drinking alcohol.

*****

Max Nogel, Grass Valley, Oregon—"I was in the Cinnabar Lounge in Prineville, having a few drinks with Mac and some of the other cowboys, when this logger wandered in off the street and announced, 'I've come to town to whip me a cowboy.'

"That was the wrong thing to say in the Cinnabar. Mac slid off his barstool and told the logger, 'Well, I'm a cowboy, and we'll just have to see if today is your lucky day or not.' They walked out the door and the fight was on. Mac was the one who walked back in.

"Another time a group of us were in the bar in Spray, Oregon. The bar was closed and the door locked. A drunk started pounding on the door, wanting to come in for a drink. Mac got tired of the noise and told the bartender, 'Can't you get rid of him?'

"'No,' said the bartender, 'Can you?'

"Mac pushed back his chair, walked across the room, yanked open the door, and when the drunk started to stagger inside, Mac hit him so hard the fellow flew back a good 10 feet and up and onto the hood of a pickup parked there.

"Mac could be feisty like that—he refused to put up with nonsense of any kind—but he was always a great friend to me. I was a roper, and when the competition dragged on late, Mac took my two kids, a boy and a girl, to the fanciest place in town and would buy 'em steak dinners. He was bighearted like that. There were definitely two sides to Mac Griffith."

*****

Larry Mahan, Sunset, Texas—"When I was a kid coming up through the amateur circuit, Mac Griffith was someone I looked up to. He was a great all-around cowboy, a natural athlete and a tough customer. I had all the respect in the world for his abilities. In my book, Mac was a good guy.

"Mac was at the tail end of the *old-time cowboys*, the men who were the backbone of the sport of rodeo. He was in the class along with men like Jim Shoulders, Casey Tibbs, and Deb Copenhagen. They were the salt of the earth; men who just went out and rode.

"My era in rodeo came on the heels of those great men. I was one of the young bucks coming in and we were conscious of the physical and mental aspects of the sport of rodeo. We studied nutrition, lifted weights, ran, stretched, studied and prepared ourselves to try and achieve better competitive results.

"Whenever I was at a rodeo and ran into Mac, he was friendly, having a good time and smiling. He enjoyed every moment and lived to the fullest. Mac was a true superstar of the sport, but he always made time for those of us who were trying to rise up through the ranks. What is interesting—I've thought about this—is that, if Mac had lived, he and I would have gone head-to-head for the World All-Around. Would I have won the title five consecutive years from 1966 to 1970, and again in 1973, like I did? Sure I would have."

*****

Bill Brewer, Powell Butte, Oregon—"I grew up on the Blackfoot Reservation in Montana. You had to learn to fight if you grew up on the reservation, especially if you were a white kid. In that kind of situation, you don't want to start at the bottom and work your way up. It's a whole lot better to find the toughest guy, and if you whip him, then the others leave you alone. That was the law of the reservation.

"In a way Mac Griffith subscribed to that rule. He thought he was the toughest. He wasn't. He was mostly big, and his bark buffaloed a lot of people who were afraid to stand up to him.

"When I started out rodeoing back in 1948, you had to be damn tough if you were going to travel down the road. You drank a lot of booze, and did your share of fighting. That was just the way it was. There wasn't any of this Christian cowboy crap—drop to one knee, poke a finger toward heaven, praise the Lord—you see on television today. Back in my day the only time the Lord's name was ever mentioned was as a swear word when you got bucked off.

"Mac was no better, no worse, than any other cowboy of that era. If a fellow couldn't fight a little, you got bullied. If you stood your ground, even if you got whipped, you earned respect. That was my experience in rodeo, and I carried a card for a lot of years."

*****

Gene Marr, Joseph, Oregon—"The Griffith family lived here in the Wallowa Valley. The boys, Mac and Don, were always messing with horses. They broke horses and worked for local ranchers when it came time for gathering or branding. They were a couple of tough kids and used to fight about every day. If they couldn't find a town kid to fight, they fought each other.

"After the Griffiths left out of here, I lost track of them. But I always did follow Mac's career on the rodeo circuit. He did himself proud. When he got killed, I never heard much about that except there was a gal mixed up in it, and Mac was in the wrong place at the wrong time."

*****

Gibb Gregg, Dayville, Oregon—"I first met Mac Griffith when we were kids riding amateur rodeos together. There was no doubt Mac was a good athlete, and a tough guy to go up against in a fistfight. He tried his hand as a professional fighter. Mac told me he thought he was tough until he stepped into the ring with real boxers, and after he got punched in the face a few times, he gave up the sport and went back to rodeo.

"Mac was the type of guy who was never far away from trouble. One year I traveled with him and three other cowboys, back to ride in rodeos on the East Coast. That was before the days of interstate freeways. We took back roads all the way, never got a motel room, just kept trading off driving and sleeping. In New York City, after Mac won some money bulldogging, he was celebrating and just for the hell of it picked up a garbage can and tossed it on top of a cop car. He got arrested. We had to pool our money, 800 bucks—a whole lot of money in those days—to spring him. We rode again the next night in Boston, and managed to win enough for gas money to get home, but that was about it.

"I was surprised when I heard Mac had been killed in a bar fight. I felt real bad because he was just coming into his prime."

*****

Betty Pedro Barnstetter, Pendleton, Oregon—"I grew up on a ranch between Pilot Rock and Ukiah. We had an arena at our place, and after World War II ended, the ranch rodeos started. A couple times a year the local cowboys showed up at our place. That was when I first became acquainted with Mac Griffith. He was young, but a good cowboy and could ride most anything.

"I knew Marilyn Porter from having gone to school with her at Pilot Rock. She quit school to marry Mac. After that I saw them only occasionally, usually at a rodeo. And then when I was living in Pendleton, Marilyn contacted me, said she was going to beauty school and wondered if I knew a place in Pendleton where she could live. I had her move in with me. The way Marilyn explained her situation was to say she and Mac were married, but it was an on-again-off-again thing. Mac was always away chasing another rodeo, but he phoned Marilyn at our apartment several times a week, usually late at night after the bars closed.

"When Mac came to Pendleton, he always expected Marilyn to party with him, and usually they insisted I go along for the ride. The three of us had a lot of fun together. Mac was good to me, respectful and even kind. He gave me a belt buckle he won in Baker City. He could be generous like that. He never held onto anything.

"One year I was at the Round-Up, and there was Mac without a buckle on his belt. I started to take off my buckle with the intention of giving it back to him, but he stopped me, said, 'No way. I gave it to you, you keep it.' I told him, 'Okay, buster, but remember, I tried. If your pants fall off in the middle of your ride, don't blame me.'

"Back in the late '50s and early '60s, if you were around the cowboy crowd, you took your life into your own hands. Mac was my protector. He had a reputation for being tough and he watched over me like a big brother. If a rowdy cowboy bothered me, Mac took care of the situation. One time at the

Ranch Club in Pendleton, Mac and Marilyn and I were eating dinner, minding our own business, and some cowboy came out of the bar to get Mac because a fight was brewing. Mac went with him. There were sounds of a huge fight with glass breaking and everything. A few minutes passed, and Mac came strolling back into the dining room dusting his hands. He sat down and finished his dinner like nothing out of the ordinary had happened.

"Mac's hands were always a mess; scar tissue on top of scar tissue, knuckles swollen, skin cut and bruised from fighting. One time I saw Mac and Neil Beemer—he owned a service station in Pendleton, and probably weighed 350 pounds—take turns slamming their fists into the dash of Neil's car, trying to prove who had the best punch and could endure more pain. All they proved was they could beat the hell out of a dash and dent it up.

"A lot of Mac's so-called friends took advantage of him. They had Mac do their dirty work. Only once did I actually see Mac fight, and that was at a bar in Heppner. It was an honest fight, fair and square. After it was over, I asked Mac why he had continued to hit and kick the man when he was on the ground. And Mac looked at me and said, "Because he'd have done the same damn thing to me." After that I never wanted to see another fight.

"If Mac was sober he was a sweet guy to be around, but if he was drinking this other person came out; cocky, loud, arrogant and aggressive. If you partied with Mac he was fun, up to a point, and when that point was reached it was obvious Mac's personality had changed. It wasn't that Mac went looking for fights. It was more that fights came looking for Mac. I remember him telling me he wished he could step away from the rat race, but he didn't know what else he could do to make the kind of money he made rodeoing.

"When Mac and Marilyn were on the outs she dated other men. She was pretty and men were not hard for her to come by. Then Marilyn and Mac got back together, she got pregnant and had a baby. I thought things were going to work out for the best, was hoping so because I liked them both.

"When Mac got killed, Marilyn called and told me, said she didn't want me to hear it through the grapevine. A lot of stories circulated about what had happened in Prineville. I heard Mac and Ronnie Raymond were flirting with some fellow's girlfriend, or ex-wife. I heard it happened in the parking lot behind the Ochoco Inn. Then a new rumor had it a car pulled alongside, and someone leaned out and shot Mac, but the bullet was meant for Ronnie. Some people even said Mac got what he deserved. That made me mad. He did not *deserve* to get shot. Sure, Mac could be wild, and he was tough, but he wasn't any different than a lot of cowboys I knew.

"I just wish Mac was alive today. If he was, and if he somehow managed to stay clear of the bars, there is no telling how good he could have been; how many World All-Around titles he would have won. We'll never know."

*****

Albert Van Dorn, Meridian, Idaho—"Back when Mac Griffith and I were rodeoing on the amateur rodeo circuit, we rode steady all summer, but come winter we had to find paying jobs to carry us through. Mac tried professional boxing. He was a hell of a good street fighter because he was big and strong and faster than most of the men he fought. But professional fighters have experience and can defend themselves. I saw every one of Mac's three professional fights. He came wading in, fists flying and all the professionals had to do was counter. Mac lost all three. They were bloody messes, with Mac the one spilling the blood.

"Mac gave up the fight game and went to work for me in Salem, selling Electro Hygiene vacuum cleaners and Fillmore sewing machines door-to-door. Mac was a big, good-looking fellow. The housewives were all too willing to let him get his foot in the door, and he had a good sales pitch, but when it came to closing the deal, Mac got bashful and had trouble asking whether they were planning to pay cash or finance. Mac starved out as a salesman, but that was okay because he went back to rodeoing.

"Some people try to paint Mac as the bully, but that's a bunch of bullshit. Don't get me wrong, Mac did like to scrap, but he didn't bully nobody. If Mac was gonna fight, he picked out the biggest son of a bitch in the bar. He enjoyed whipping the toughest guy in town. That was just Mac.

"One time four of us were on our way to a rodeo down south and we stopped in Burns, Oregon—actually it was Hines, at the Antlers Bar—to have a steak dinner and a few drinks. We shot shuffleboard until our dinners were ready, and then sat down and ate. Four local men came in and started playing shuffleboard. Buzz Seely, a bronc rider out of Grandview, Washington, was traveling with us and he went over and backhanded the pucks off the shuffleboard table and into the gutter. Buzz was famous for pulling crap like that, especially if Mac was around to back him up. Buzz and one of the locals went outside to square off and Mac warned the other three it was going to be a fair fight, and not to step off the sidewalk. One of the men made the fatal mistake—took a step—and Mac growled, 'He's mine.' He decked that fellow, and the other two. It took a blink of the eye and Mac cleaned house. After that, we stood and watched Buzz fight the first guy. Buzz couldn't fight his way out of a wet paper bag.

"Mac drank to socialize, and have a good time; we all did. If you were in rodeo you drank a little. Mac sure as hell was never a *hard drinker*. To me a *hard drinker* is a guy who can't get out of bed in the morning unless he has a bottle in hand. Mac was never like that.

"Mac was one to flirt with a pretty girl—sure he was—it was his lifestyle. Most of the chasing he done was just to see if he had what it took to get a particular gal in the sack. It was the challenge of the thing, not the doing of the thing, that appealed to Mac. After all, Mac had Marilyn waiting for him at home, and she was a pretty special lady.

"In my book Mac Griffith was a real friend and a hell of a good guy. That's all I've got to say."

*****

Rich Raymond, Mt. Vernon, Oregon—"Mac Griffith and my brother, Ronnie Raymond, were great friends—two peas in a pod. They went full bore at anything they ever done.

"Mac could be a real prick when he was drinking. Once in Portland, at the PI, we were drinking in the Red Steer, and Mac zeroed in on me, wanting to fight me. I got tired of his bullshit, reached in my hind pocket, whipped out my billfold and laid 500 bucks on the bar and told Mac, 'Tell you what I'm gonna do.' I patted the money on the bar. 'Match this, we step outside, the man who walks back in takes it all.'

"Mac went over to talk to my brother, wanting to know if I was serious. Ronnie told him, 'Hell yes, he's dead serious, and if you take him up on it you're gonna be 500 poorer and beat to shit.' Mac pulled in his horns, said he wasn't gonna fight me, told me to put away my money. He bought me a drink. After that, I never had an ounce of shit out of Mac Griffith. I found out early in life, if you stand up to a bully, nine times out of ten they back away. Was Mac a bully? He could be if he thought he could get away with it.

"As far as what happened when Mac got killed, all I can say is what my brother told me. I was working for day wages, riding for Gil Cattle Company near Paulina, and wasn't in town that night or I would've been smack dab in the middle of it all. That night in the Cinnabar, there were two groups drinking and having a good time; Mac, some cowboys and a few locals at the bar, and a couple of state cops and their friends, at a table. A woman got mixed up in things, Mary Edgerly. She caught Mac's attention and the two of them made eyes at each other and danced to music on the jukebox. She was the one who cranked up the fight, got things rolling. That's what I was told.

"One thing led to another, and Mac squared off with a state cop, Larry Irwin. They went outside to fight. My brother,

Ronnie, and another cowboy, Jimmy Bothum, figured Mac would handle the state cop and be back in a moment to buy a round of drinks. When Mac didn't come back, Ronnie and Jimmy went to look for him and I guess they found Mac beat to hell. He had been worked over with a sap or something. About then this local mechanic, Duane Harvey—he had been married to Mary Edgerly—drove up in his car. Larry Irwin, the state cop, jumped up and tried to run away, but Ronnie chased him down. Harvey got out of his car and pulled a pistol. Mac was in no condition to do anything. He was draped over Jimmy's shoulders. Harvey pointed the pistol at Mac and pulled the trigger. Mac went down. Then Harvey went over and threatened Ronnie with the gun, and Ronnie ran back in the bar and called for an ambulance. When it got there, Mac was dead. That's about all I know.

"Ronnie got subpoenaed for the trial, but he damn near wasn't alive to testify. Quite a bad snow storm blew in right after Mac got killed. Had a hell of a lot of snow on the ground and then a big Chinook followed and we had the worst flood in the history of Eastern Oregon. Cattle were scattered everywhere and Ronnie came to Paulina to try and help me get the cows to higher ground. He was riding on the lower flat, along the Crooked River where the banks drop off seven or eight feet. A cow tried to break away. Ronnie went after her. The bank gave way, and the horse he was riding, a real nice sorrel gelding, fell into the water. They were swept downstream in the current, to where a sheet of ice, six or eight inches thick, covered the river. Ronnie came up under the ice. He had to dig with his fingernails and inch himself along until he found a pocket of air and was able to catch a quick breath. He kept going, pulling himself under the ice, going from one little air pocket to the next, until he reached the edge and was able to get his feet under him. He climbed up the bank—not an easy thing to do—and it was still a couple mile walk to the ranch house. By the time he got there, his clothes were frozen as stiff as a board.

"After the water went down, I found the horse in the river and got the saddle off. The horse, in its panic trapped under the ice, must have pawed off the bridle and that was a dirty rotten shame because it had a hell of a nice Garcia bit. I took the saddle home, dried it out and rubbed Neatsfoot oil into the leather. Ronnie rode that saddle for a lot of years.

"All of us cowboys were wild back in those days. We got drunk and fought. It was just that Ronnie and Mac would hang onto a drunk a little longer than the rest of us. Those two were special. They were the first American cowboys to win at Calgary: Ronnie won saddle bronc and Mac bulldogging. They won despite those Canadians being pretty territorial and cliquish. They got paid with cash and a trophy, a bronze sculpture by C. A. Biel. Ronnie sold his trophy and it made me madder than hell that he did; sold it to rodeo announcer Mel Lambert for chicken feed. Mel turned right around and resold it to the Bank of Edmonton for 54 grand. That's the way it was in those days, easy come, easy go.

"The first cowboy I knew to take up flying to rodeos was Marty Wood, but Ronnie was right behind him. One time Ronnie rented a plane to fly to the Paulina rodeo. The wind was blowing pretty hard that day and Ronnie misjudged, came in a little hot, and couldn't make the landing strip. He tried to pull up, but hit a wheel on the ticket booth, took the roof off and he crashed the plane in a rock pile. Was one hell of a wreck, and when the dust settled, Ronnie came crawling out of what was left of the plane with a fifth of whiskey in one hand and a smile plastered across his face like he had enjoyed the ride.

"Like I said, we all could be a tad fun-loving and free-wheeling back in the day. I do know, Ronnie and Mac could have both been World Champions, if they could have left the booze alone. Mac flamed out early. Ronnie lasted a while longer. To his dying day the one thing that always stuck in Ronnie's craw was the unfairness of the trial for Duane Harvey, the fellow who shot Mac Griffith. Ronnie claimed the state cop, Larry Irwin, lied on the stand, that things didn't happen the way he said they happened, and that the defendant never told the truth either. Jim Bodie, the defense attorney, changed things around and made it look like Ronnie and Mac were some sort of dangerous desperadoes, and the only choice Duane Harvey had was to pull the trigger. According to Ronnie, that was a crock of shit."

*****

Bill Nichols, Prineville, Oregon—"I was living at Paul's Trailer Court in Prineville. Mary Edgerly lived in a trailer right across from me. Nearly every morning I'd wake up and either Ronnie Raymond, or his brother, Rich, would have their rig parked beside her trailer. Guess they took turns; something like that.

"It was breaking day the morning of December 16, 1964, when Tex King, the sheriff of Crook County and a personal friend of mine, came wheeling in and stopped at my trailer. Tex knew my background as a rodeo rider, and the first thing he wanted to know was about Mac Griffith. I said I knew him, asked why he wanted to know. Tex said, 'He got shot last night.' I said, 'Serves the son of a bitch right. He had it coming.' That was all Tex needed to hear. He wasn't the least bit interested in how I came to have that opinion.

"Mac Griffith was an ornery sucker; apt to put his cigarette out on your plate while you were eating, steal your drink, knock off your hat. He'd mess with you until you fought him. That was Mac.

"One time I was at a dance. There was a good lookin' gal sitting between Mac and his brother, Don. I didn't know she was Don's wife and I asked her to dance. Mac came unglued and challenged me to an arm wrestle contest. I danced first and then arm wrestled Mac. It turned out he couldn't pin me, and I couldn't pin him. It was a draw. But that didn't settle nothin'. It was obvious a fight was brewin' and I thought it best to get the hell out of there. I headed for the 86 Club in Redmond.

"Mac and Don, and some of their friends, high-tailed it to Redmond with the intention of catching me at the 86 Club. I got sidetracked and was late getting there, but it just so happened my brother, Ray—we were both big, strong boys and looked just alike—was there. The cowboys jumped him. By the time I walked in, it looked like a wrecking ball had gone through the joint; chairs busted, broken bottles, blood everywhere, and Mac, Don and the others were laid out like cordwood on the floor. All my brother said was, 'The tougher they are the better I like it.'

"After that, whenever Ray and I were at a rodeo and ran into Mac and Don Griffith, they always kept their distance. They were never quite sure which one of us had whipped 'em."

*****

Sammy Flynn, Dayville, Oregon—"I ain't got even one good word to say about that rotten son of a bitch, Mac Griffith. I rodeoed with him, but he sure as hell was never a friend of mine. When I was maybe 15 years old—back then I went a hundred and a quarter wringing wet—Mac got after me down in John Day. I wouldn't fight the bastard on account of he was a lot bigger and stronger and woulda killed me. After that, whenever Mac seen me, he picked on me. He was an asshole.

"Mac could ride broncs okay, and then he got to ridin' bulls and made a name for himself. Why the hell was he so famous? All he ever won was the big four twice, and the only reason he done that was because he scared the piss out of the judges. Mac picked on small men. Men his size he left alone. Mac Griffith was chicken shit.

"The night Mac got himself killed there was a woman who wanted to get back at her ex-husband and she figured Mac would kick his ass. It was a shameful thing, but it came to a good end because Mac was the most overbearing asshole I ever was around. If ever a man deserved a good killing, it was Mac Griffith."

PART THREE

Douglas Shepard
(Oregonian *newspaper February 3, 1965)*

The District Attorney

Douglas "Doug" Shepard was born in 1931 and raised on a farm near Tumalo, in Central Oregon, a place where open range was the law of the land, the sport of rodeo was king and hunting season was reason enough to close schools. Doug joined the U.S. Army during the Korean War, was honorably discharged and used his G.I. Bill to gain a degree in political science from the University of Oregon. He was not sure how to use his degree, and toyed with the idea of moving to Washington D. C. and finding a job with the government. He ultimately decided in favor of remaining in the Northwest, and his logical path seemed to be in pursuing the legal profession. He graduated from Northwestern Law School (Lewis and Clark College) and passed the Oregon Bar in 1962. He was recruited by attorney Ralph Brown to come to work in his Prineville office.

"When I arrived in Prineville, there were only three attorneys," said Doug. "In addition to Ralph Brown, there was Jim Bodie, and Jim Minturn, who split his billable hours between private practice and being the part-time district attorney.

"As far as the community, it didn't take long to discover the makeup of Crook County was a diverse mix of cowboys, loggers and sawmill workers. The three factions didn't blend especially well together.

"Another interesting layer of the social fabric of Prineville was what was generally regarded as the *John Hudspeth factor*. Hudspeth was a lumberman who owned timberland and a saw mill and was one of the most prominent men in town. He had moved to the area in the late 1930s and brought along with him a workforce from Oklahoma and the Southern states. These folks had a certain way of thinking, and if one of them happened to be seated on a jury, their mindset was that, *he had it coming,* was a valid defense in almost any situation."

Doug Shepard was busy trying to build his private practice when, on December 9, 1964, Jim Minturn abruptly resigned as Crook County District Attorney and joined Jim Bodie in his law practice. Less than a week later, Mac Griffith was shot and killed. On January 9, 1965, Governor Mark Hatfield appointed Doug Shepard to take over the duties of the part-time Crook County District Attorney. He had only three weeks to prepare the case against Duane Harvey, the man charged with murder one in the shooting death of Mac Griffith. Getting a guilty verdict would be a big challenge for the new prosecutor.

"When I stepped in, the murder investigation was pretty much complete," said Shepard. "What I pieced together from the information available was that John Hudspeth and some other locals, a group of cowboys and two off-duty Oregon State Officers, had been drinking in the Cinnabar Lounge and were involved in an altercation. The outgrowth of this dispute led to one of the officers, Larry Irwin, getting in a beef with a cowboy, Mac Griffith, and they agreed to step outside the bar and fight.

"Griffith was a tough character, but so was Irwin. They both had experience as professional athletes: Griffith as a professional rodeo cowboy and boxer, and Irwin as a professional baseball player. The upshot of their fistfight was that Irwin beat the tar out of Griffith, just hammered him. Now Griffith might very well have killed Irwin if he had got his hands on him, but Irwin danced around, kept his distance, and peppered Griffith with punches until he knocked him down and then continued to pummel him.

"Duane Harvey, a local mechanic and an Air Force veteran, had been drinking in the bar that night. His ex-wife, Mary Edgerly, was there also. I don't know Harvey's motivation for leaving the bar, but he did. He got in his car and drove around the block to the city parking lot behind the Ochoco Inn. When he arrived, the fight between Irwin and Griffith was over. Griffith was on his feet, but staggering and being helped along by his cowboy friend, Jim Bothum. Harvey produced a weapon, a derringer, and warned Griffith to stay away, to not come any closer, and then *bang* he shot him. One shot was all it took. The bullet struck Griffith in the midsection and he went down. As this drama was unfolding, maybe 30 paces away, Ronnie Raymond had come out of the bar and was beating on Larry Irwin.

"After shooting Griffith, Harvey walked over to where the fight was going on between Raymond and Irwin. He pointed the double-shot derringer at Raymond and warned him he would pull the trigger; something to that effect. In response Raymond jumped up and ran. He returned to the bar, informed the bartender, Pat Leonard, there had been a shooting and instructed her to call an ambulance. Meanwhile, Harvey helped carry Irwin to Harvey's car and they sped away, leaving town.

"And that, in a nutshell, was my case. Initially Harvey was charged with murder one, which requires proof of premeditation. Upon hearing the evidence, the grand jury reduced the charge to murder in the second, which requires the prosecution to prove murder, but not premeditation to commit that murder."

The Crook County District Attorney did not rate an office in the courthouse and Shepard had to pack the investigative files to the downtown office he shared with Ralph Brown. They did not have a secretary or a law assistant; they were on their own. When Shepard was not working on his private practice, he prepared his case to prosecute Duane Harvey. Since it would be a major trial, with important implications as far as establishing his law career, Shepard requested outside assistance from the Oregon Attorney General. Fred Robinson, a deputy district attorney from Josephine County was assigned to the case. According to Shepard, "Robinson was as green as I was. He had never tried a murder case and had very little experience as a prosecutor. He was good for moral support, but very little else."

Duane Harvey had retained the services of Jim Bodie, a veteran attorney, and Jim Minturn, the former district attorney. Shepard had glowing words to say about his adversaries, especially Jim Bodie.

"Bodie was a damn fine attorney," said Shepard, "one of the best around. He was feisty and cagey, and put a lot of emotion into arguing a case. He was from the South, and in the courtroom his Southern drawl became more and more pronounced as he went along. He performed like an actor; should have won an academy award for his lead role in the Harvey trial. He was every bit as charming and convincing as Atticus Finch in *To Kill A Mockingbird*.

"I cut my eye teeth on Bodie and did he ever give me an education. I learned more from him in one trial than I did from all my professors at law school. Judge Foley, an older man and an experienced judge, presided over the Harvey case, and over my objections he allowed Bodie to interject testimony into the trial that had no business being admissible. He allowed Bodie to turn the barroom brawl into a free-for-all, and muddy the waters with conflicting testimony. He allowed Bodie to assassinate Griffith's character, to make the victim the bad guy. The trump card Bodie played was the one that allowed *'he had it coming'* as a legal defense for killing a man. Let's just say this about the Harvey trial; Bodie pulled every trick in the book and did what he felt he had to do to win the case.

"I never should have lost the Harvey trial. But, in my inexperience I made some tactical blunders. I failed to put enough emphasis on the fact the victim was 20 feet away when

Harvey pulled the trigger, and after the shooting Harvey acted like a guilty man, a man who knew he had done wrong and tried to hide the evidence. He drove Irwin to Bend that night, and along the way he hid the derringer pistol, the murder weapon, in a juniper tree. Jesus, if that does not demonstrate a culpable mind! I should have hung my hat on that guilty action, Harvey getting rid of the gun.

"Judge Foley allowed testimony to be admitted about an incident in a bar where someone broke a beer bottle over Griffith's head and it never even fazed him. Another witness testified he had been eating dinner with his family in a restaurant in Prairie City and Griffith spit on his plate. When the fellow got to his feet Mac hit him and caused permanent brain damage. Anyway, the guy swore he hadn't been *right in the head* since Mac hit him. What did any of that have to do with Harvey pulling the trigger? Absolutely nothing; except to build in the jury's mind that Mac was a mean man, and if he got you on the ground, he was likely to maim you, or kill you. That's what Bodie wanted the jury to believe. I think he was successful. Should it have been a part of the Harvey trial? In my opinion the answer would not just be *no*, but *hell no*.

"One mistake I made in presenting the prosecution was in reenacting the shooting. I was Harvey and my assistant, Fred Robinson, was Griffith. I pointed my hand at Robinson, said, 'bang' and Robinson fell to the floor like he had been shot and lay there twitching. I did it for dramatic effect, but the response I got from the jury was not what I expected. They were amused. There were even a few chuckles. If you are a prosecuting attorney presenting a case, you do not want humor in the courtroom. The demeanor in the courtroom should be very solemn and dignified. If the jury is amused it diverts attention away from the seriousness of the crime. They are less likely to bring back a conviction.

"In closing statements, the prosecution is always up first, then the defense, and the prosecution has the opportunity for a final rebuttal. When it was Bodie's turn, he got up in front of the jury and went into the same old song and dance—it had been Harvey's duty to kill Mac Griffith because he was such a bad guy—and he poured it on so thick with his South Carolina twang you could have cut the words with a knife. Bodie worked himself into a fever pitch—he broke into tears, real tears—threw up his hands, told Judge Foley he was unable to continue, and motioned for his assistant, Jim Minturn, to take over. When Bodie stormed from the courtroom we sat in baffled silence, listening to his footfalls thunder down the stairs. It was all very staged, very theatrical, and I must add, very effective.

"Minturn took over. He was cool, calm and collected. Even though he had been in court each and every day, sitting beside Bodie at the defense table, he stated he considered himself to be, more or less, a neutral party; representing himself as being akin to the 13th juror in this case—like he was an impartial player!—and began to doggedly go over the evidence, plowing the exact same ground Bodie had already plowed, hammering it into the jurors' heads. His argument was that Harvey had acted in self-defense to save his own life and that of another, Larry Irwin, the state cop.

"Then out of left field, Minturn introduced the name of Kitty Genovese, a young woman who was murdered in New York City while dozens of witnesses stood by and did nothing. The story had been front page news for weeks, and was even featured on the cover of *Time* magazine. Minturn had the nerve to superimpose the Kitty Genovese case on the Harvey case, blatantly stating that in New York City nobody came to the aid of that poor girl as she was being brutally raped and murdered, but by God, the citizens in Crook County came to the aid of their fellow man. He called Harvey a hero, and said if he had fought in the war and performed such a courageous act, he would have received a medal. The jurors were on the edges of their seats. They listened intently, captivated and spellbound by every word of Minturn's brilliant performance.

"In my rebuttal I should have done a better job of countering Bodie and Minturn. Their entire case was based on redirecting the blame from Harvey and placing it squarely on the broad shoulders of Griffith and his disreputable reputation. It made sense. Hell, they were trying the case in Crook County; home of a vigilante uprising where five men were hung off the bridge south of town; home of the Sheep Shooters' Association, a group of cattlemen responsible for slaughtering thousands upon thousands of sheep during the range wars a half-century before. The defense was banking that the community would be of the opinion, if you had a bully, it was best to take him out behind the woodshed and work him over. My approach should have been to say something to the effect that in South Carolina, *he had it coming,* might be a legal defense but not in Crook County, Oregon. I should have explained how the citizens of Crook County had wrestled this land away from the Indians and brought civilization along with them. In a civilized society we have laws we must live by. We obey those laws. Taking another man's life is not okay. It is the most serious of all crimes. I should have said something like that, but I didn't.

"It's not that I tried a bad case. I did my best. I made mistakes, things in hindsight I wished I could have done differently. My inexperience was costly. What did I learn about presenting a case to a jury? I learned that the hard, cold facts can be misconstrued and distorted and twisted. A case is won on appearance, psychology and the skill of an experienced attorney to convince a jury.

"When the Harvey jury came back with their verdict so quickly, I wasn't particularly shocked because Bodie and Minturn had pulled out all the stops. Where I lost a conviction was in trying Harvey on a second degree murder charge only. I should have included a list of lesser charges and allowed the jury to pick and choose. If they couldn't convict him of second degree murder, perhaps they would have convicted him of intentional manslaughter, unintentional manslaughter, or involuntary manslaughter."

*****

"It was maybe 20 or 25 years after the trial that I was in Redmond, sitting in the lounge at Mrs. Beasley's, having a cocktail," said Shepard. "Ronnie Raymond and some cowboys came in and sat near me. Ronnie must have pointed me out, that I was the prosecutor who failed to get a conviction in the Harvey case. One of the cowboys stood up, came over to my table, and in no uncertain terms he informed me I had been bought off, had thrown the case against the man who killed Mac Griffith, and right then and there he was going to kick my ass. Ronnie managed to pull the cowboy out of the bar before there was any serious trouble. But I sat there thinking to myself, what a hell of a thing it is in our society when a fellow does his best, and a couple of decades pass and some drunk wants to kick his ass in a bar.

"Now I hear one of the witnesses, Larry Irwin, confessed on his deathbed, saying the defense got him to lie on the stand, and his testimony supposedly swung the jury to decide on a not guilty verdict. Soliciting false testimony is a crime; a felony. Bodie and Minturn were a couple of old war horses, battle tested, and what might very well have happened was that while Bodie was interviewing Irwin, certain things were put into words, and Irwin was smart enough to repeat those words when he testified. I won't put something like that past Bodie, not to say he was crooked, or would do something unethical or illegal, but Bodie was the type of individual who, if he saw an opportunity to take advantage of a situation, might very well have taken it.

"During the Harvey trial, if I had known there was even a hint that false testimony had been solicited by the defense, I would have pondered how best to use that information to my advantage. More than likely, I would have set a trap for Bodie, and if he had been overconfident and wandered into that trap, I would have sprung it on him. But, after all the time that has passed, what Larry Irwin had to say on his deathbed is strictly hearsay. It doesn't matter anymore.

"If I had the opportunity to try the Harvey case today, I would hope the outcome would be far different. I would like to think I could get a conviction. I truly do believe Duane Harvey deserved to be put in jail."

The Defense: Jim Bodie, Duane Harvey, Jim Minturn
(Oregonian *newspaper, February 3, 1965)*

The Defense

James "Jim" Bodie was born and raised in the small town
of Clinton, South Carolina, the first state to withdraw from the
Union and join the Confederacy. Some of that same rebellious
spirit was in Jim's lifeblood as he raised himself up from very
humble beginnings. His father was an alcoholic, and to help
support the family, Jim worked in the cotton fields. He joined
the Army, served in England in the Quartermaster Corps
during World War II, and came home and applied the G.I.
Bill to gain his undergraduate degree from William and Mary
College. He ventured west to attend Willamette Law School
in Salem, Oregon.

Jim Bodie maintained his very distinctive southern drawl
and slow, deliberate mannerisms. He never seemed hurried
or harried. He wore a suit to the office each day and gave
the impression of being unflappable. He championed for the
underdog and the downtrodden, and in the courtroom came
across as fiery as a Baptist preacher. On rare occasions, when it

benefited him the most, he was emotional to the point of crying genuine tears. Bodie was rational, sensible and personable, but he could also be moody, neurotic, obsessive and overbearing. At trial, he insisted on being the one in control; the same way a puppeteer controls all aspects of the puppet show. Bodie was a natural at grasping the big picture—able to take a very complex issue and quickly reduce it to understandable terms—but he was less likely to be involved in details. It was almost as if mere minutiae were beneath his intellectual ability to comprehend.

Jim Bodie and Jim Minturn became friends while attending Willamette Law School. After Bodie established his law practice in an office space above Prineville Men's Wear, he called Minturn and asked him to be his partner.

"I know why he wanted me," said Minturn. "I enjoy the process of putting the pieces of the puzzle together. I am logical, methodical and very detail oriented."

*****

Jim Minturn was born in 1926, grew up in Salem, and graduated from Willamette Law School, passing the Oregon Bar in 1951. His first job was as an attorney-auditor for the inheritance tax department of the Oregon State Treasurer's office. He resigned to join Jim Bodie in his law practice, and arrived in Prineville, on the first day of February, 1954. Within a few months the Crook County District Attorney, Vernon Burda, unexpectedly resigned, and Oregon Governor Paul Patterson appointed Minturn to the post of part-time district attorney. In total, Minturn served 10 years in that capacity, before resigning on December 9, 1964, to concentrate on his expanding private practice. A week later, Duane Harvey gunned down Mac Griffith.

"The Harvey case fell in our lap," said Minturn. "Pat Taylor worked as the secretary in our law office. Her father, Cy Taylor, was the Justice of the Peace, a job Pat eventually assumed, but the important point was that Pat had been married to Duane Harvey. After his arrest for murder one, she felt sorry for Duane, and begged Bodie to take the case. He consented and asked me to help him with the defense.

"Harvey was being held in jail, and we arranged to have him released on $5,000 bail. He came to our office to tell his side of the story and I found him to be very forthright in telling the events that led up to the shooting. But his memory about the actual shooting, and his reactions in the aftermath, were not very good. Bodie and I had to constantly prompt and prod Harvey to have him recall specific details.

"I began pouring over the police reports relating to the shooting and interviewing witnesses who were in the Cinnabar the night of the shooting. I also interviewed a wide range of people who frequented the bars in Prineville. It quickly became evident that the victim, Mac Griffith, was not only a famous cowboy, but also a notorious barroom brawler. As my investigation unfolded, I interviewed a number of people who had witnessed fights where Griffith was a participant, one of which had taken place in Prineville when Griffith put two loggers in the hospital with severe injuries."

Bodie made a bold announcement to the press, claiming the defense would not contest the fact Duane Harvey had shot and killed Mac Griffith. He claimed Harvey's justification was self-defense. But Minturn, with his unique perspective as a former prosecutor, had serious doubts that Harvey was an innocent man.

"Bodie was absolutely convinced that Harvey had acted in self-defense," said Minturn. "But I had doubts, questions and concerns. Why had Harvey felt compelled to drive to the parking lot where the fight was taking place? He stood outside his vehicle; then got back inside to retrieve a gun, and used that gun to kill Griffith. It was my contention that a reasonable man, when confronted with a dangerous situation, would simply leave the premises as quickly as possible. But Harvey chose to stay, and in making that choice he escalated the situation and placed himself in a position where he made the choice to take a very aggressive action. At such a point, the balance between an act of self-defense and an act of murder is very tenuous, very tenuous indeed.

"I was concerned about the distance between Harvey and Griffith when the shooting occured. By Harvey's own admission, Griffith was seven or eight paces from him. I had to question if such a distance posed an imminent danger, and whether Harvey was justified in taking the actions he took. I wanted to know why, from a distance of 20 or 25 feet, Harvey felt his life was in peril, especially considering the fact Griffith had received a severe beating in a fistfight, and had not yet had time to recover his faculties.

"Also disturbing me was in trying to understand Harvey's actions and activities following the shooting. He drove away with Larry Irwin, the police officer who had been involved in the fistfight with Griffith, and on the way to Bend, Harvey hid the gun he had used, placing it in the branches of a juniper tree. That spoke volumes to me; that Harvey knew he had done something wrong, and was trying to distance himself from the weapon and his involvement in the shooting."

Bodie patiently listened to his partner express his considerable doubts about Harvey's innocence. Then Bodie stood, went to the bookshelf where he kept his Oregon Revised Statutes, chose a particular volume, pulled it free and packed it to the table where he set it down with a resounding thud. He licked a forefinger and pawed through the pages until he came to ORS statute 161.209. He read aloud the legal description of self-defense. "A person is justified in using physical force upon another person for self-defense, or to defend a third person from what the person reasonably believes to be the use, or imminent use, of unlawful physical force, and the person may use a degree of force which the person reasonably believes to be necessary for the purpose." He slammed the book shut, tapped the gunmetal gray leather-bound cover with a forefinger and announced, "Mr. Harvey was not only protecting himself, but was coming to the aid of his fellow man. His actions saved his own life, as well as the life of Larry Irwin. This is a classic case of self-defense."

Once again Minturn brought up Harvey's guilty actions in the aftermath of the shooting—hiding the gun—but Bodie scoffed, said that could easily be explained by Harvey being scared. He said a jury could relate to those actions, and would not hold that against Harvey. But Minturn continued to play the devil's advocate, pointing out the weaknesses in the defense and the discrepancies between the police reports and Harvey's memory of what happened. He said the prosecutor would have a field day with the fact Mary Edgerly, Harvey's ex-wife, had been in the bar that night, dancing and flirting with Mac Griffith. He proposed Harvey might very well have killed Griffith in a jealous rage. And while that possibility lay exposed as a potential risk to the defense, Minturn once again returned to the fact Harvey had had every opportunity to leave the scene but had chosen to stay and confront Mac Griffith.

A moment of awkward silence fell between the two men—a dangerous silence, similar to placing a finger too close to the gears of a worm drive and tempting fate—then Bodie threw up his hands and began restlessly pacing the room. He stopped, whirled and snapped, "Jim, you worry too goddamn much."

Bodie, as if suddenly becoming weary, sat down with a groan, placed his elbows on the conference table and ran his splayed fingers through his thinning hair. In a calm voice of reason and justification he said, "Our defense will concentrate on the fact Mac Griffith was a bad man who liked to fight with his fists and hurt people. Harvey was well aware of Griffith's reputation; knew if the *cowboys* got him down, he would likely be beaten to death."

From the way Bodie growled the word *cowboys*, it was evident he considered them to be an inferior breed, a subspecies, uncivilized and unfit for society. Motioning with his hands for added emphasis, Bodie resumed his discourse, "Harvey was an innocent bystander, a peacemaker, and he acted to protect his own life, as well as that of a police officer. Self-defense— black and white—and according to Oregon law, Harvey was completely within his legal rights to take the action he took. We have a great defense.

"The overriding fact of this case is that Doug Shepard will be trying his first major case as the new district attorney. He's as green as grass. I have tried hundreds of cases, and you were the district attorney for 10 years. We will overwhelm Shepard with our experience." Bodie, smug with confidence, was grinning. Any tension that had existed between the two attorneys ticked away in the intervening silence like an over-driven car ticks away its heat. Bodie and Minturn were united, a team, and together they would defend Duane Harvey to the best of their combined abilities.

*****

"I did the bulk of the investigative work in putting together Harvey's defense," said Jim Minturn. "But in the courtroom, Bodie was the kingpin while I sat beside him and took notes. Once in a while Harvey jotted down something pertaining to a fact, or a discrepancy in someone's testimony, but mostly he sat unmoving, looking morose, all too aware of the gravity of the charges he was facing, just as he had been instructed to act. Harvey's mother attended the trial. We made sure she was seated in the front row. She was a sympathetic figure for the jury to see, continually crying into a handkerchief she kept clutched in her hands."

One witness, John Hudspeth, was served with a subpoena as he sat in the Cinnabar Lounge, but he promptly tore up the paper, tossed the pieces in the air and vowed to never set foot in the courtroom. He never did, and no legal action was taken against him to force him to appear.

As the trial got underway, Bodie continually sought to bring out the aggressiveness of Mac Griffith's personality and how dangerous he became when he was drinking. He also demonstrated through his cross-examination of witnesses, the other cowboys at the Cinnabar Lounge the night of the shooting—Ronnie Raymond and Jim Bothum—were cut from the same bolt of cloth as Mac Griffith. The witnesses who were called to the stand were extremely guarded in their testimony.

They certainly did not want to incriminate themselves in any way. Oftentimes the testimony of one witness conflicted with the testimony of another. At those times, Bodie seized the initiative and attempted to play up the discrepancies and the overall confusion that existed in the Cinnabar the night of the shooting. He made it seem as though the bar was a hornet's nest, a very chaotic place that could erupt in violence at any moment.

The prosecution based its case on jealousy. Testimony was given that Mac Griffith had made sexual advances toward two women, Pat Leonard, the barmaid, and Mary Edgerly, the ex-wife of Duane Harvey. Harvey was romantically involved with both women. The district attorney sought to prove Duane Harvey killed Mac Griffith in a jealous rage.

"Shepard built his entire case on the jealousy factor," said Minturn. "In my opinion that was a fatal mistake. There were many other more plausible issues that concerned Harvey and his actions that night. Why was Harvey there in the first place? Why did the prosecution never probe Harvey's level of perceived threat, his sense of imminent danger, his ultimate decision to discharge a weapon? What about his guilty actions after the shooting? Shepard failed to exploit, or to even question any of these. And it was interesting to me that Shepard never examined Duane Harvey's alcohol consumption. That was never brought into question even though he had been drinking for at least five hours and was more than likely intoxicated. Did alcohol cloud his judgment and decision making? Another thing, why did Harvey return to his car and arm himself with a derringer when he just as easily could have driven his car the short block to the police station and report that a man was being beaten? There were a host of factors which contributed to the killing, and none of these were explored and exploited by the prosecution. Why not? In my opinion, the answer is simply that Shepard was too inexperienced in the courtroom, especially when he was pitted against an aggressive attorney like Jim Bodie. Shepard placed all his eggs in one basket, and then failed to prove they were eggs.

"But the biggest blunder of all occurred when Shepard and his assistant, Fred Robinson, attempted to reenact the shooting. They stood in front of the bench, facing each other at a distance of six or seven paces. Shepard pointed his finger at Robinson and said *bang*. Robinson fell to the floor with a thud. They were like a couple of kids on the playground. I saw members of the jury grinning and trying not to laugh. A titter raced through the audience and forced Judge Foley to rap his gavel to regain order in the courtroom.

"I talked to a friend, an attorney from Bend who had come over to watch the trial, and he said when he saw how the jury reacted to the demonstration of the shooting, right then and there, he knew Harvey would be acquitted. Humor certainly never puts a jury in a convicting mood."

The prosecution rested and the defense began its case with Bodie hammering it into the minds of the jury that Mac Griffith was a vicious man. And while he assassinated Griffith's character, he heaped praise on Duane Harvey, pointing out his favorable service in the Air Force, his tendency to be a peacemaker, and the courage he exhibited in standing up to the bullying cowboys. He skillfully avoided answering why Duane Harvey felt a compulsion to drive to the parking lot where the fight was going on, place himself in harm's way, and shoot a defenseless man from a distance of at least 20 feet away. He dodged the possibility that jealousy could have been a contributing factor. And he downplayed Harvey's guilty actions following the shooting.

A major turning point occurred when Larry Irwin, the state police trainee, was called to the stand. His testimony was crucial to the defense. If he was weak and failed to support a clear and present danger, the jury was likely to convict Harvey.

"At that point there was no doubt about it, Bodie was in charge and was directing all aspects of the trial," said Jim Minturn. "Bodie was at his best cross-examining the State's witnesses, pulling from each witness what would be most advantageous to the defense, and not allowing testimony to be introduced which might prove beneficial to the State."

As Bodie charged ahead, Doug Shepard seldom objected, even when it was obvious Bodie was leading a witness down a primrose path. The exchange between Bodie and Larry Irwin began with Bodie asking Irwin if he had started the fistfight in the parking lot behind the Ochoco Inn. Irwin testified that Griffith threw the first punch. Bodie then asked Irwin to describe the fistfight in his own words and tell what happened after the conclusion of the fight—how two of Griffith's friends, Ronnie Raymond and Jim Bothum, had come to the parking lot, and how Irwin had tried to escape.

At the conclusion of Irwin's remarks, Bodie asked, "You were on the ground and Ronnie Raymond was hitting you. Is that correct?"

"Yes, that's correct."

"You felt threatened, didn't you?"

"Yes, I did," answered Irwin. "I didn't know how many of them there were."

Bodie said, "You thought you were going to die, didn't you?"

Irwin nodded his head in agreement and muttered, "Yes, I did. I thought they were gonna kill me."

Bodie seized that information like a dog with a bone. "That's when you shouted, 'Help! Help! They're killing me! They're killing me!' And Duane Harvey pulled the trigger because he thought they were going to kill you. Duane Harvey had the personal courage to step in and save your life, didn't he? You cried, 'Help! Help! They're killing me! They're killing me!' Do you remember saying those words?"

Larry Irwin picked up on Bodie's lead. "Yes, that's what I said."

"Repeat what you said so members of the jury can hear you," instructed Bodie.

"Help! They're killing me!" repeated Irwin.

Bodie turned to Judge Foley and said, "I have no further questions for this witness." Larry Irwin was excused from the stand.

*****

"That is pretty much how I remember that particular exchange in the courtroom between Bodie and Irwin," said Minturn. "If I had been sitting at the prosecution's table, I most certainly would have strenuously objected. It was obvious, from the manner in which he framed his statements and questions, that Bodie was directing the witness. But Shepard did not object.

"Now it has come to light that Larry Irwin stated on his death bed that he felt Bodie forced him to make statements on the stand that were not true. I don't know about that, but you have to understand, Larry Irwin was a state cop, a trainee, and he had been drinking in a bar, got in a fistfight, and his opponent was subsequently killed. Irwin was in deep trouble, and in his testimony he was attempting to justify his actions during the fistfight, as well as afterward when he fled the scene of a crime.

"As a courtroom attorney, Bodie had an aggressive style and I can see where someone might get the impression he directed a witness to obtain specific information from that witness. But I do not believe Bodie purposely directed a witness to lie on the stand. If he had done such a thing, it would have been a prosecutable crime."

*****

During the defense's closing argument, after Bodie had stormed from the courtroom, Minturn took over. And although such a switch is almost unheard of in a courtroom setting, it was a planned tactical maneuver perpetrated by the defense. Bodie thought Minturn would provide a *calming influence*, and had directed Minturn to take over and again explain the details of the case, and to finish strongly with the Kitty Genovese comparison they had discussed in graphic detail.

*****

When it was announced the jury had reached a verdict, Jim Bodie returned to the courtroom. The not guilty decision was read and Bodie leaped to his feet, stuffed all the scattered papers on the table in front of him into his briefcase and bolted from the room. Harvey, who seemed stunned at his acquittal, stood without showing any outward sign of emotion and allowed his family and friends to hug him. Jim Minturn remained in the courtroom and as he shook hands with Doug Shepard, he felt a cold tightness in the pit of his stomach, knowing the young district attorney had tried his best, but had failed.

"Prosecution is a hard job," said Minturn. "The prosecutor wants to establish intent and to show the perpetrator in the worst light possible. The defense wants to confuse any intent, and show the defendant in the best light possible. When I was a prosecutor, and an acquittal was presented, I felt as though justice had not been served. If I got a conviction, I felt sorry for the individual who was going to jail. As a prosecutor, or a defense attorney, all you can do is present the best case you possibly can. It then falls to the jury to render its collective decision.

"If I had been the district attorney prosecuting the Harvey case, and had all the facts in front of me, I would say that Duane Harvey, definitely and without a shadow of a doubt, got away with murder."

Pat Leonard testifies on the stand
(Oregonian *newspaper, February 3, 1965)*

The Bartender

Pat Leonard had graduated from Crook County High School in 1949, along with her classmate Duane Harvey. She married young, was divorced from her husband, Stan Leonard, and coped as best she could with being a single mother. In 1964, Pat was 33 years old and had worked at a variety of jobs around Prineville. She took the evening shift bartending at the Cinnabar Lounge because it allowed her the flexibility to spend days with her daughter, Linda, and with tips added in, it was the best paying bartending job in town.

Pat dated several men, including Duane Harvey. Duane had served overseas in the Air Force during the Korean War. He spent several years living in Japan and was teaching Pat the fine points of eating with chopsticks. When they went on dates, they generally stayed in town, had a few drinks at the Casino Bar, east of town, and ate at the adjoining Chinese restaurant. Pat described Duane as, "A good guy, average height and weight, and although there was nothing really remarkable

105

about him, I did enjoy his company and the stories he shared about the places around the world he had visited."

On the evening of Tuesday, December 15, 1964, Pat arrived for work at the Cinnabar Lounge a few minutes before 6 p.m. She was not expecting anything out of the ordinary, just the normal assortment of loyal customers who frequented the watering hole, a part of the mythical Ochoco Inn. The lounge was a narrow room, dimly lit with blue lights, except for the back bar where a harsh white light illuminated rows of bottles, alcoholic beverages arranged by brand name and type. The Cinnabar had a reputation as a tough bar, but according to Pat, the Casino attracted a much rougher crowd. There were fights at the Casino several times a week, but fights at the Cinnabar were infrequent. If she had trouble in the bar, Pat knew better than to call the cops. They took their sweet time responding, as much as three or four hours, and yet the police station was only a block away. When the cops did arrive, whatever trouble had been brewing had long since boiled over and resolved itself.

"Tex King was the county sheriff," said Pat. "My dog would have made a better sheriff than Tex King. The city cops weren't any better. I always knew that if trouble broke out in the bar, I was on my own."

When Pat started her shift that evening, she had a single customer. Mac Griffith was in the bar drinking call gin, Tanqueray, and mixing it with Seven-Up. Judging from how much gin was left in the bottle, Pat figured Mac had been drinking for the better part of the afternoon. In the past, she had served Mac on many occasions. Whenever he visited town he made it a point to stop at the Cinnabar Lounge, known in rodeo circles as a *cowboy bar*. Mac could hold his liquor like few other men. He never gave the appearance of being inebriated.

"When Mac got drunk he raised his voice and became belligerent, crude and coarse. That is when I knew he was drunk," said Pat. "When Mac was drunk, he either told me I was pretty and asked me for a date, or he made vulgar sexual suggestions. That night he pestered me; telling me he had a room at the hotel and inviting me to come there after my shift and spend the night with him. Mac was a handful for any woman."

Pat was well acquainted with cowboys, the local variety and the traveling cowboys who often stayed at the Ochoco Inn and frequented the Cinnabar. Pat said, "Mac was famous, but I served a lot of famous cowboys. I kept an eye on Mac. He had a reputation as a fighter, and I didn't want fighting in my bar. If the place got broke up, I'd more than likely lose my job. I knew that."

Over the first several hours of Pat's shift, a few locals drifted in and drifted out. Around 9 p.m. Duane Harvey stepped into the bar and took a seat at one of the tables. Mac remained at the bar. When Pat served Duane, she dallied for a few minutes, exchanging pleasantries. She was friendly with Duane. Upon her return to the bar, Mac demanded to know, "Who's that son of a bitch?" He nodded toward Duane Harvey. "What makes him so special?" Pat never bothered to answer.

"Mac certainly took notice when Duane showed up," said Pat. "Every once in a while he looked in Duane's direction and shouted, 'I can whip anybody in this bar.'

"Duane pretty much ignored Mac, but each time I brought Duane a fresh drink he would make a disapproving comment; asking why I didn't kick Mac out or saying I should call the cops. His comments were loud enough Mac could hear, and I told Duane to hush. I didn't want trouble and certainly didn't want Duane to get hurt. I became so irritated with Duane that I reprimanded him, saying, 'I don't tell you how to mechanic, don't tell me how to run a bar. Mac is just being Mac. I can handle him. Keep your opinions to yourself.'"

About 10 p.m. Mary Edgerly came into the Cinnabar wearing a full-length beige raincoat, buttoned all the way up. Pat had never seen her at the Cinnabar before, but frequently saw her at the Casino. Mary was a petite woman, very pretty, with an extremely nice figure that she liked to flaunt. She had been married to Duane Harvey, but they had divorced. Duane stood and offered Mary a chair at his table. As she sat, Duane motioned to Pat and bought Mary a drink.

After she finished that drink, Mary stood, twirled, and in an enticing voice she boasted, "Under this coat all I have on are my baby doll pajamas." Her hands were on the buttons of the coat, and it appeared, with a little encouragement, she might be willing to prove the point.

Pat reacted quickly, stepping out from behind the bar, she said, "Fine, honey, just make sure you keep that coat on and buttoned up tight as a Christmas package."

Mary frowned, as if an intimate pleasure had been denied her, and with her lips pouting, she sashayed to the bar, claiming a stool near where Mac was sitting. She used both hands to smooth the overcoat hiding the baby doll pajamas, and she arched her back as she swung up and onto the high stool. She crossed her bare legs very deliberately, turned and flashed Mac a dazzling smile. Mac had missed none of her enticing performance and he grinned and addressed Mary, saying, "Hello, darlin'."

Mary flirted with Mac. He bought her a drink, and then another. They talked. He patted the empty stool beside him, inviting her to move closer. She did. He tried to kiss her, a clumsy attempt, and she pushed him away, admonishing him with, "Slow down. We have all night."

Mac got up and fed coins into the jukebox, avoiding any song by the Beatles—*I Wanna Hold Your Hand; She Loves You; Hard Days Night; Love Me Do.* Mac did not like the Beatles; he did not like their long hair. He asked Mary to dance. She accepted. They danced close, first to Dusty Springfield singing *Wishin' and Hopin','* and after it finished they stayed on the small dance floor while the jukebox whirled, changing songs, and then they danced to one of Mac's favorites, Roy Orbison singing *Pretty Woman.*

While the couple was busily engaged, swaying to the music, three casually dressed men entered the bar—Larry Irwin, an off-duty Oregon State Police trainee stationed in Bend; Ron Crawford, an off-duty Oregon State Police trainee stationed in Prineville; and Jerry Hubbard, a Bend variety store manager and former Marine—and they took a table in the adjoining room, the Rustler's Roost. They ordered food and a pitcher of beer. A few more customers came in: Lee Rhoden, a local rancher; Don Chase, owner of the Hay Creek Ranch; Bob Clark, a cattle buyer from Portland; Jack Christensen, owner of a Portland meat packing plant; and John Hudspeth, owner of the Hudspeth mill and logging operation. They occupied a table in the bar. When the Rustler's Roost closed, the two cop trainees and the ex-Marine, having finished their dinners, moved to the bar. They sat at a table near the locals and ordered more beer.

A pair of well-known cowboys arrived ahead of the local crowd of drunks who wandered in every night after the taverns closed at 1 a.m., having a beer or two before staggering home. Pat was well acquainted with the cowboys. She had served them on many occasions and liked them both. Pat said, "Jimmy Bothum was a bronc rider from the Willamette Valley, a nice guy who behaved himself. He was a sidekick to Ronnie Raymond, a champion bronc rider from Paulina, who might well have been the toughest man in Prineville. If his brother, Rich, was with him, they were double tough. But Ronnie was always a gentleman around me.

"My customers kept me busy serving drinks. The jukebox was playing. People were talking. I didn't stand around and listen to what was being said, but everyone seemed to be getting along. I didn't see even a hint of trouble. The cowboys were at the bar, Mary with them. Everyone else was gathered around two tables. All of a sudden John Hudspeth raised his voice and jumped to his feet. Duane jumped up too, and as he did, he picked up a chair and heaved it in the direction of John Hudspeth. He missed John, but hit Bob Clark, slicing open his head. Duane chased John toward the bar where Ronnie Raymond slid off his stool, grabbed Duane by an arm and told him, 'Leave him alone. He's an old man.'

"Then Larry Irwin got involved and pushed someone. A drink spilled or was thrown. There was more pushing and shoving and the next thing I knew, Larry Irwin and Ronnie Raymond were on the floor wrestling. Ronnie was on top. I yelled for them to knock it off; to take it outside."

Don Chase pulled Ronnie Raymond to his feet. Mac Griffith wrapped his arms around Larry Irwin so he could not swing. Things settled down. Pat went to check on Bob Clark. His scalp wound was bleeding freely and she handed him a bar towel to use as a compress. Someone bought the house a round, and Pat was kept busy distributing drinks. Mac continued to sit at the bar with Mary Edgerly. Every so often he swiveled on his stool to announce to the room in a loud voice, "I'm the toughest son of a bitch in here," and sometimes shouting, "Only one thing I do better than ridin' an' fuckin'—that's fightin'."

Pat recognized Mac had had too much to drink. She cut him off and refused to serve him the drink he had coming. She poured the drink that was in front of him into the sink.

Larry Irwin called to Mac, inviting him to come to the table where he was sitting. Mac blustered, "Ain't no coyote in me," and joined the group, but quickly tired of their company and returned to his stool, finding Mary Edgerly was gone. He mumbled, "Where the hell did she go?" The question was not directed at anyone in particular.

"I was headed to the bar when Larry Irwin stepped up to Mac," said Pat. "I overheard him say, 'We might as well finish this thing.' What he said didn't immediately register with me, not for a few seconds. Once I realized they were going to fight, I told them to take it outside. Mac stripped off his coat—he was wearing a nice leather jacket—folded it neatly and laid it over the back of a chair. Someone asked Mac where he was going and he smiled and replied, 'To teach this cop a lesson.' The two men walked out the door, Mac following Larry Irwin. A couple of minutes passed and I think it was Jimmy Bothum who asked about Mac, where he was, and I said, 'Him and that state cop went outside to fight.'"

With that announcement, the bar emptied in a headlong rush as patrons, eager to see a fistfight, poured out the door and onto Main Street. Pat quickly locked the doors behind them, gathered the money from the till, and took the cash to the hotel desk so the receipts could be locked in the safe for the night. She went back to the lounge to clean the tables and the bar.

"Someone pounded on the back door," said Pat. "I unlocked it and Ronnie Raymond came bursting in, out of breath, huffing and puffing, shouting, 'My God! They shot Mac! Quick, call an ambulance!'

"I made the call and went outside to view the situation and see if there was anything I could do. When I got to the parking lot, a small crowd was standing around where Mac was lying face down on the pavement. Mary Edgerly was tugging on one of his arms, trying to get him to stand. I told her to leave him alone. Mary turned Mac onto his back. There was blood on his face and blood coming from his ears, but he was breathing, moaning some. I thought to myself, at least he's alive. We waited for the ambulance. It seemed to take forever. It was cold. Jimmy Bothum became impatient and tried to bust out the driver's side window of Mac's car with his fist, but the glass didn't break. It wouldn't have mattered because Jimmy didn't have a key. But nobody was thinking. We were all just standing there in shock. Mary sat on the pavement and put Mac's head on her lap. We waited some more and finally a cop did show up, and not long after that the ambulance arrived and took Mac away.

"That's about all I know. What struck me as unusual, was how fast everything escalated; from the fight breaking out inside the bar, to Mac being shot. The blink of an eye, it seemed to me.

"I knew exactly what had gone on in the bar because I was there and witnessed it. What happened in the parking lot, I really don't know, but I can guess.

"My guess is that Mac and Larry Irwin walked outside, down Main Street, turned the corner and went to the city parking lot. I have to assume Larry Irwin hit Mac with something besides his fist, a blackjack maybe. I say that because I was told about the time Mac was riding a horse and got bucked off into a steel pole. They thought he had to be hurt and took him in for an x-ray. The doctor who looked at the x-ray said Mac had an unusually thick skull that protected him. Yet, the coroner who examined Mac after he was pronounced dead, said he suffered a severe concussion. Larry Irwin wasn't that big. I don't think he could have knocked Mac down without some help. Maybe he used something, or maybe his friends sitting in the bar with him that night circled around and joined in. I don't know. I have a lot of questions and no good answers.

"The day following the shooting, Mr. Bodie called me at home. He said he was representing Duane Harvey and he asked me to come to his office. I went to his office and sat at a conference table. Mr. Bodie placed a recorder in front of me with the microphone pointed in my direction. He told me to tell him what happened. I named my customers who had come to the bar the night of the shooting, said what they were drinking and how much they had had to drink. I tried to give an accurate picture of the situation and the events as they occurred. Mr. Bodie allowed me to talk, until suddenly—for no reason as far as I could tell—he reached over and turned off the recorder. He said, 'I'm not going to make a tape of this.' He punched the button to rewind the tape and told me to leave.

"Doug Shepard, the district attorney, also had me come to his office and explain the events that led up to the fight and the shooting. He was a nice guy, but young. He said this was his first big case and that he had never before been involved in a murder trial. He took notes and seemed very interested in my relationship with Duane Harvey. I told him we had been on a few dates. He wanted to know how many. I said I didn't know. He pressed me for a number. I guessed maybe a dozen. He asked if Duane was protective of me, if he considered me to be his girlfriend. I laughed, said it wasn't like that, not at all. We were friends, and once in a while we went out for drinks or to dinner. That's what I told him. But Mr. Shepard wouldn't leave it alone and kept asking me personal questions. I answered them to the best of my ability."

The prosecution subpoenaed Pat Leonard, and at the trial she joined the other witnesses sequestered away from the courtroom. The witnesses were instructed not to discuss their testimony or say anything about the case. Pat talked a little to Jimmy Bothum, but mostly she sat quietly, waiting for her name to be called so she could testify and go home to her daughter.

"When I did take the stand, both Mr. Shepard and Mr. Bodie went after me tooth and nail," said Pat. "Mr. Shepard wanted to make it seem as though I was the focal point and that Duane killed Mac over me. He tried to claim jealousy was the motive. And Mr. Bodie wanted me to say Mac was this terrible person. Neither was true.

"During his cross-examination, Mr. Bodie insisted I repeat the exact words Mac had said to me. I really didn't want to say that in court, but finally I did repeat the words, 'Why don't you let me rear up on you?' And Mr. Bodie acted like he was unsure what that phrase meant. He asked if Mac wanted to have sexual intercourse with me. I answered, 'I'm not exactly sure, sir, but I would suppose that was what he was driving at.'

"Mr. Bodie became very aggressive, asking if I was aware Mac Griffith became extremely violent when he was drinking and oftentimes engaged in fistfights that put his opponents in the hospital. I answered I was well aware of Mac's reputation. Mr. Bodie abruptly turned away from me, and I was excused from the stand and allowed to leave."

*****

"I found the legal process to be extremely disappointing," said Pat. "They never gave me the opportunity to tell my story of exactly what had happened in the bar that night. The attorneys kept interrupting me, and it was up to the judge to determine whether or not I could continue to talk, or if I had to restrict myself to certain elements. The district attorney certainly did not impress me. It seemed as though Mr. Bodie was running the courtroom. If other witnesses were treated like I was treated, and not allowed to testify properly, then justice was not served. The shooting was not over jealousy, or anger, not in my opinion. But when I heard the verdict I was shocked. I really thought Duane would get jail time."

*****

"About a month after the trial, Duane called and asked me to dinner," said Pat. "We never talked about the shooting, not until Duane pulled into my driveway at the end of the evening and I blurted out what was on my mind. 'Duane, tell me what happened.'

"He got all teary-eyed and cried for a long time. He told me, 'Not now, but someday I'll tell you, I promise.'

"I never saw Duane again, but my take on what happened that night is this; Duane had been drinking. I know he was drinking before he came in, and I know how many I served him. He went to the parking lot and the fight was over. Mac was there and so were Ronnie Raymond and Jimmy Bothum. Duane got scared and thought he was going to get his ass kicked. He pulled the trigger. Alcohol, fear, poor judgment; a man died. I'm still puzzled by it all."

Larry Irwin
(Oregonian *newspaper, February 3, 1965)*

The Oregon State Trooper

Larry Olen Irwin was born February 28, 1938, in Chickasha, Oklahoma. His grandmother, on his father's side, was Cherokee Indian.

"Our family lived in Indian territory until coming to Portland, Oregon, in 1943. Dad worked in the shipyards during the war," said Monte Irwin, three years younger than his brother, Larry. "Dad was a strict disciplinarian. He had had some amateur boxing experience and wanted his boys to be able to stand up for themselves. He built us a makeshift gym with a heavy bag and a speed bag. Most every day, Larry and I strapped on boxing gloves, and Dad taught us to fight. Mom was very religious and peace loving; adamantly opposed to fighting. We fought in spite of her objections."

It was evident from a very early age that Larry was a gifted athlete. He graduated from Pleasant Valley Grade School and attended Milwaukie High School, where he was popular and excelled at all sports, especially baseball. He was chosen as the starting pitcher on the American Legion All-Star Team, and baseball scouts touted him as one of the best major league prospects to ever come out of the Northwest.

When Larry reached the legal driving age, 16, he bought his first car; a 1950 Chevrolet, two-door, with an automatic transmission. He was good at art, took painting classes, and at home incubated pheasant eggs and raised them to turn loose because he liked to watch the roosters strutting around the property. But it was the game of baseball where Larry really made his mark. After graduating from high school in 1956, he signed with the Boston Red Sox and was given a substantial signing bonus.

The Red Sox sent Larry to their rookie league team in Waterloo, Iowa. The day before the opener—in which Larry was to be the starting pitcher—Larry and five other *bonus babies* were riding around in a new convertible drinking beer. The driver was speeding, failed to navigate a corner, lost control and the car overturned in a corn field. All the occupants were thrown out. The car landed on Larry, crushing his left shoulder and coming to rest on his head. One of the ballplayers, a big Italian kid, lifted the car, freeing Larry. He was rushed to the hospital.

"When Larry came home his left arm was paralyzed, just hanging down, nothing more than skin and bone," said Monte Irwin. "The Red Sox thought he was finished, but Larry was determined and worked out for a solid year, proving them wrong by coming back stronger than he had ever been. Mace Brown, the legendary pitching coach for the Red Sox, had Larry work out for him and he said Larry was as fine a right-hander as he had ever seen. And Mr. Brown had certainly seen some mighty good pitchers in his time.

"Larry didn't throw a sidearm curveball. He came down over the top, numbers high and the ball dropped out of sight. Nobody, but nobody, could hit that pitch. And Larry had a fastball which actually sizzled when he turned it loose—102 miles per hour—all but impossible to see. When he turned it loose, all you heard was that sizzle, and the sharp pop when the ball hit the catcher's mitt."

In his third year of professional baseball, Larry was assigned to the Red Sox farm team in Albany, New York. There was talk the Red Sox were planning to bring him up, use him as a reliever in the big league, but that never happened. Larry's arm gave out, and the Red Sox gave up on him. He came home and went to work with a friend as a carpet layer.

"When Larry's baseball career ended he was disappointed. It had been his dream," said Monte. "But he got on with life.

"The two of us were close to the same size and weight. I was a little bigger, six-foot, 180 pounds and more muscular and rawboned than Larry. We fought for the fun of it, and I want to emphasize this and cannot say it strongly enough, Larry had a right hand like stone. He had the best right hand I was ever hit with.

"Dad was there watching one of our fights. Larry and I were standing toe-to-toe, trading punches. I caught Larry with a left hook and his right eye immediately swelled shut. It staggered him. I threw my right. He ducked and threw his right—*the hand of stone*—and the flesh under my left eye peeled back and my broken nose was flattened off to one side of my face. I went down. Larry figured it was over and started to walk away. I came to my senses and went after him. He knocked me down again, and this time when I got on my feet, he was 40 feet away with his back to me. He must have heard me coming because he turned and hit me in the solar plexus with that right hand. After that, I didn't have enough wind to go after him again.

"The only person who ever whipped me was my brother. In my estimation, Larry stood 10 feet tall. He was a mighty man. I say that because I don't know anybody who could outperform him—in athletics, a fistfight, a shooting contest, debate, painting a picture—he did everything better than anyone else ever could. I followed in Larry's big footsteps. I tried to live up to the example he set."

Larry and Monte served in the Army during the days of the Cold War. Larry was sent to Korea and assigned to an elite, top-secret unit armed with a rifle-mounted nuclear warhead, the *Davy Crockett*. This three-man team patrolled along the

DMZ with the world's smallest nuclear device, capable of delivering a warhead equal to 20 tons of TNT and emitting a deadly circle of radiation.

Monte served as a personnel specialist during the Cuban Missile Crisis, and when he was discharged, he began working as a trainee for the Oregon State Police assigned to the Pendleton office. A few months later, when Larry was discharged, he joined his brother as a trainee with the Oregon State Police and was assigned to the Bend office.

"At that point in our lives, Larry and I were on top of the world," said Monte. "We held respectable jobs, had spending money in our pockets, fast cars to drive and nice clothes to wear. Our future was bright. We had it made; anyway I thought we had it made up until the morning of December 16, 1964. Sergeant Armstrong, the head of the Pendleton Oregon State Police, called me into his office. He asked where I had been the night before and if I was with my brother in Prineville. I said I had been in Pendleton. I wanted to know why he was asking, and that was when I first learned Larry had been in a fistfight and that a man was dead.

"I asked permission to go see my brother," said Monte. "I followed that by saying, with or without Sergeant Armstrong's permission, I was going, even if it cost me my job. Sergeant Armstrong gave me the time off, but he warned me I was to stay away from trouble. I fired up my Ford Crown Victoria—'55, pink and white, chrome bar over the top, big block that could really pick it up and lay it down, absolute top of the line—and headed south for Central Oregon, bucking a blizzard all the way. I made it through by tucking in behind a semi-truck, and letting him bust through the snow drifts. It took me 12 hours to go from Pendleton to Prineville, and when I pulled into town I found out the grand jury was convening in the courthouse. I went there, found Larry, and after the hearing, we talked. He told me the details of exactly what had happened the night of the shooting.

"Larry said he went to the Cinnabar Lounge in Prineville with two other guys; his roommate, Jerry Hubbard, and

Ron Crawford, a state police recruit stationed in Prineville. They had dinner and a few beers. According to Larry, he was recognized as a state cop and some of the patrons in the bar started making derogatory statements about the state police. John Hudspeth, a local mill owner, got a fight stirred up between Larry and a cowboy, Ronnie Raymond. It was mostly a wrestling match, no big deal, over and done with quickly.

"When trouble came knocking, Crawford and Hubbard bailed. They went for coffee, leaving Larry to fend for himself. The barmaid told Larry she didn't want trouble, and didn't want to see him get hurt. She warned him, if there was a fight involving the cowboys, it wouldn't be a fair fight and advised Larry he should leave. But Larry didn't know how to back away from trouble. He tried to smooth things over, and he even invited the cowboys to join him at his table. He bought a round for the house just to show there were no hard feelings.

"But then one of the cowboys, Mac Griffith, out of the clear blue, challenged Larry to a fistfight. They went outside, squared off in the parking lot behind the hotel, and Larry allowed Griffith to swing at him three times before he gave him that famous straight right *hand of stone*. One punch knocked Griffith off his feet and onto the ground. Larry knew about Griffith's reputation as a fighter, and thinking the other cowboys in the bar were going to gang up on him, he wanted to make sure Griffith was out of the way. Larry kept hitting Griffith in the face so he would pass out. But Griffith was hard-headed. He wouldn't go unconscious.

"Two of Griffith's cowboy friends, Ronnie Raymond and Jim Bothum, showed up and tried to pull Larry off. Larry hit Bothum and knocked him back and out of the action. Larry got up and tried to get away, but Raymond chased him down, tackled him and managed to get on top. He was kicking him in the head with his cowboy boots. Larry remembered hearing a gunshot. He said it sounded like a pop, and the next thing he knew Duane Harvey was telling Raymond to get off. Harvey dragged Larry to his feet and they got away from there.

"Larry went to the hospital in Bend, had to get stitches, and was missing a couple teeth. He called his sergeant at home, told him what had happened, about the fight, and that a man had been shot. Larry was put on administrative leave pending an internal investigation, and a few days later he was unceremoniously fired.

"My brother was fearful that the beating he administered to Mac Griffith might be called into question, but he was never charged with any crime. I did not come back for the trial, but Larry was subpoenaed as a material witness. According to Larry, the shooter, Duane Harvey, was represented by Jim Bodie, and he was a very wise old turkey of an attorney. My brother described Jim Bodie by saying he was a *one-man army*.

"Larry was an excellent witness on the stand. He was good-looking, well-dressed, and came across as intelligent, truthful and convincing. Of course, Larry was sad Griffith had been killed, and he was fearful Duane Harvey would get the death penalty for having pulled the trigger. Larry felt as though the damage had already been done. That's what he told me.

"After he testified, Larry called me and he was still emotional. One thing he said was, he felt as though Griffith, if he had lived, posed a greater threat to society than Duane Harvey ever would. In saying what I'm about to say, I realize I'm damaging my brother's reputation, but I'm not a liar, and I'm not an exaggerator. It's time the truth came out, all of it.

"When Larry was on his deathbed, dying of cancer, he told me Jim Bodie coached him to say, 'Help! Help! They're killing me! They're killing me!' But Larry never said those words. That was a contrived statement. It was not true. Yet Larry testified to that in court. And that was the turning point in the trial. Larry's testimony allowed Duane Harvey to walk. Why did Larry do it? Maybe he felt Duane Harvey was not a cold blooded murderer. What happened that night happened in a split second and you have to ask yourself, should a man have to pay for that split second for the rest of his life? I don't know. I just don't know."

*****

Larry Irwin, after being terminated from his job with the Oregon State Police, returned to the Portland area and resumed his former career as a carpet layer. He settled into a life of owning and driving fast cars, partying and raising a little hell when the mood struck him. He walked a fine line between being a law abiding citizen and being a lawless renegade, just as Mac Griffith had often done.

"The same year as the trial in Prineville, 1965, Larry and I were drinking at a spot called The Grove, on 112th and Powell," said Monte. "There was a big fellow in the bar wearing a Batman T-shirt. I don't know why I did it. I should have left him alone, but I teased him about his shirt. The man took offense, as he should have, and we went outside and fought. I knocked him down and thought it was over. I was heading back inside when Larry yelled at me to look out, but it was too late. The guy jumped me. I had learned some wrestling moves, and managed to flip the big guy over on his back. I gave him my best shots. He got to his hands and knees and Larry was hollering at me, *'Finish him off!'* But I knew the guy was hurt—hurt real bad. I refused to inflict any more damage. I walked away. Larry was disgusted with me; he called me a chicken shit.

"The man was taken to the hospital and remained in a coma for four days and nights. I sweated it out, thinking if he died, I could be charged with murder. It turned out the fight fell under a clause in the Oregon Revised Statutes known as *mutual combat*. According to the law, if two men agree to fight, and one of the participants is injured, there can be no fault levied, and no recourse brought against the other person. The man recovered, but I felt terrible for instigating the fight, and then having my own brother mad at me because I didn't *finish him off*.

"A few months after that incident, I met Larry at the Flower Drum, a bar at 82nd and Foster Road. I mentioned to Larry that I was thinking about pulling up stakes and moving to California. Larry had been drinking, and my news set him off. He claimed I was deserting him. He left the bar in a huff and got in his car. He was driving a muscle car deluxe—fire engine red, 1966 Super Sport, four on the floor hitched to a big block 396—and burned rubber up Foster Road. The cops got to chasing him—had maybe 20 cop cars in pursuit—but Larry's Super Sport was so much faster, and he was such a good driver that he got away. Then, just to taunt the cops, he doubled back and allowed them to catch him. He was charged with multiple offenses including speeding, running stop signs, reckless driving and eluding a police officer. But Larry had friends in high places. He got off scot-free. Larry always thought the laws a normal person was required to live by didn't necessarily apply to him. That was how he felt. As a result, he was given several DUI citations, and found himself on the wrong side of the law a number of other times.

"I tell these stories, not to say bad things about my brother, but to show who he was, and what it was in Larry's character that made him stand up to Mac Griffith in the parking lot that night in Prineville. From what I've heard about Griffith, and what I know for a fact about Larry, the two of them were a lot alike. They drank and they fought. That's what they liked to do. And when Larry drank, he was Jekyll and then he was Hyde. His personality changed; from what I hear it was the same with Mac Griffith. Why did those two square off? Because neither was willing to back down or give an inch. It was not in their makeup to ever take a step back. They were like two gunslingers meeting in the street. To be the man you thought you were, or the man you wanted to be, you made your stand, and you lived or you died.

"And now Larry is gone. He died of lung cancer in 2008. I have stage IV colon cancer. I don't have long to live, but I don't fear death. I believe in the Bible, and that book tells me I'll have eternal life if I believe in Jesus Christ, who gave his life for me and was resurrected. I have taken Jesus Christ into my heart and my entire being. I have asked him to be my savior. I believe my sins, which are many, have been forgiven. My brother, Larry, found that same peace before he died. He was remorseful about Griffith's death, cried about it, and wished they could have settled their differences on a level playing field. What it all boils down to is this—the state cop refused to take a step back, and the king of the cowboys didn't want to lose his crown. It was as simple as that.

"I love my brother with all of my heart. Many times I put my life in his hands and would do the same if he were here now. My love for him cannot be explained, only felt. Larry's shortcomings were alcohol and what Dad always preached to us; to never walk away from a fight.

"When I get to heaven and meet Larry we're not going to go drinking and fighting and chasing women; no we're not. We'll hug and be happy to celebrate eternal life with our Lord Savior, Jesus Christ."

Jim Bothum
(Oregonian newspaper, February 3, 1965)

The Eyewitness

James (Jim) (Jimmy) Franklin Bothum was born on a Kansas farm—a neighbor lady was the midwife—on September 23, 1940. He joined a family that included seven brothers and three sisters. After the end of World War II, the family gave up on Kansas and moved to the Willamette Valley in Oregon, settling on a small farm near the community of St. Paul. Having farmed with horses in Kansas, the Bothum brothers got involved in the local St. Paul rodeo, competing in the wild horse races and later in the rough-stock riding events.

Jim was a natural bronc rider. He was built slight, with long, lean muscles as strong and durable as braided rawhide. A man had to be physical if he was going to ride broncs, and in his heyday as a rodeo cowboy, Jim's world revolved around bronc saddles, flank straps, rosin bags, Ace bandages, athletic tape, fancy chaps with inlaid silver initials, colorful boots with buckaroo heels, shiny spurs and coal black cowboy hats. When it came his turn to ride, Jim was only conscious of bending his knees, pointing his toes out, holding the braided rein high, giving a quick nod, "Turn me loose!" and the chute gate popping open to announce a wild explosion from the bronc, rowels flashing and ripping across rock hard shoulder muscles, and the all too familiar piston-pounding jolts of the horse. The rodeo arena was a perilous place for a man to try and earn a living, but Jim topped that by hanging around with an even more dangerous breed of cowboys; men who drank to excess, fought with their fists and chased around. Jim was never much of a fighter. He fought when he had to; those times his cowboy buddies needed backup, but mostly he went about the business of being a rodeo cowboy and avoided trouble.

"The night Mac Griffith got killed I was right in the middle of the whole damn mess," said Jim. "Mac had come in town because, on a previous trip, he bounced a hundred dollar check at the Cinnabar Lounge, and he had to appear in court. He went before the judge, gave him a thousand dollar check—money he borrowed from the Christensen brother's rodeo stock contractors—and the judge directed Mac to stay in town until the check cleared the bank the following day. Mac took a room at the Ochoco Inn, and he thought as long as he had to wait for the check to clear the bank, he might as well have a good time. With Mac it was any excuse for a party.

"Ronnie Raymond and I came to Prineville. We were staying with Ronnie's mother. She lived a few blocks from downtown, and we walked to the Cinnabar, got there around midnight. There were customers in the bar, but it wasn't crowded like it sometimes got. Two state cops, Larry Irwin and Ron Crawford, were sitting at a table with another fellow drinking beer. I didn't know them, but we met and shook hands. Duane Harvey was there. I knew him. We weren't friends. He wasn't a cowboy.

"Mac was sitting at the bar. Mary Edgerly was with him. She was a pretty gal, short, really well built and had brown hair she kept fixed real nice. She was coming on to Mac, and it didn't take long to see Harvey wasn't happy about the situation. He had been married to Mary, and I think he was jealous of the attention she was paying to Mac. Harvey kept raising his voice and I had the feeling he was trying to stir up trouble, hoping someone else would fight his fight. Back in those days, the 1960s, Prineville was the type of town where, if you did want to pick a fight, there were sure enough guys around who would damn well test you; all hardworking men in top shape, big and strong.

"It was Harvey who pushed John Hudspeth until the old mill owner had a belly full of the bullshit and pulled a knife. That wasn't like Hudspeth, to pull a knife, but he did, waving it around. A chair was thrown, some blood got spilled. It was Mac who took the knife away from Hudspeth. Harvey should have thanked Mac, but he didn't.

"Mac and I had spent a lot of time together, having just returned from several weeks traveling to rodeos. We drove Mac's white Oldsmobile 98—a real fancy car—to shows on the East Coast. There were four of us cowboys on the swing to Toronto, New Jersey, Chicago and St. Louis. I placed in saddle bronc at St. Louis and Toronto. Mac won bareback and saddle bronc at St. Louis, bulldogging in New Jersey and the Saddle Bronc Championship in Chicago. Mac and Ronnie Raymond had won at Calgary in 1963; Mac bulldogging; Ronnie riding saddle bronc. They were the first American cowboys to win there. Mac came back and won the Big Four Rodeo award for the second year running, winning the All-Around at Ellensburg, Lewiston, Walla Walla and Pendleton. He was in the top 20 All-Around money winners in the world. We were flying high, all of us were, and nothing could bring us down. That's what we were thinking that night."

Mac Griffith and Larry Irwin, when they stepped outside to fight, drew little attention. The patrons in the bar continued to drink, and when Jim questioned where Mac had gone, and was told he was fighting the state cop, Jim and Ronnie Raymond quickly exited the bar and rushed to the parking lot.

"When we got there the state cop, Larry Irwin, had Mac on the ground. He was sitting on top, punching Mac in the face and slamming his head against the pavement," said Jim. "It sure as hell surprised me to see Mac down. Nobody, but nobody, knocked Mac off his feet. And right then I knew the cop had a weapon, probably a sap or something in his hand. I couldn't see it, couldn't tell for sure, but suspected he must have.

"I tried to pull Irwin off, but he popped me with a straight right that hit my left shoulder like he had swung a maul. It knocked me straight back. I staggered a couple steps and landed on my butt. It was a hell of a shot he hit me with. I thought my shoulder was busted. Then Irwin jumped up and high-tailed it, trying to run away, but Ronnie chased him down, caught up to him by the hotel loading dock—maybe 40 or 50 feet away—and tackled him. Ronnie gained the high ground and was thumping on Irwin pretty good.

"I got Mac to his feet. He was wobbly, couldn't stand on his own from the beating he had absorbed. He slung an arm around my neck and held onto me. We started to make our way in the direction of Mac's Oldsmobile, parked on the far side of the parking lot. I was gonna take him up to the hospital. He was beat up bad and needed medical attention.

"Duane Harvey came wheeling into the parking lot in his car and slid to a stop. He got out, came around to the front in the headlights and just stood there surveying the scene. There wasn't much to see; Mac was draped over me, and Ronnie was off to the side whaling on Irwin. For some reason, Harvey got back in his car, and when he stepped around to the front again he was holding a small pistol in his right hand. In the glare of the headlights I saw the glint of the stainless steel barrel and the pearl handle grips. Mac must have seen the gun too because he mumbled, "Put that away, or I'll shove it up your ass." He was slurring his words.

"Harvey stood maybe 20 feet away, raised his hand and leveled the gun in our direction. He never said a goddamn word, just looked straight at us, and pulled the trigger. Sparks flew out the end of the barrel. I heard the bark of the report and the whomp when the bullet hit Mac. He groaned, doubled over, grabbed at his stomach with both hands and started to go down. I couldn't hold him, not with my bum shoulder I couldn't. I let him down slow, laid him on his side on the pavement. Then Harvey was in front of me waving that little gun in my face, yelling at me to stop the fight or he was gonna shoot me. I ran over to where Ronnie had Irwin on the ground and I yelled, 'He shot Mac! Clear out!' Ronnie jumped to his feet and ran for the back door of the Cinnabar, pounded on the door until someone let him in.

"I saw Irwin get in Harvey's car. They drove away real fast. A crowd gathered around where Mac was lying. We stood in the cold, waiting for the ambulance and the cops to get there. After the ambulance hauled Mac away, Ronnie and I walked to his mom's house, got Ronnie's car and drove to the hospital. We never did get to see Mac. They kept us in the waiting room, and after a while a nurse came out and said they had pronounced Mac dead. I couldn't believe it, just couldn't believe Mac was dead. That night, if we had known where Harvey had gone, we probably would have hunted him down and evened the score."

*****

"During the trial they kept me, and the other witnesses, in a side room and said we weren't supposed to talk among ourselves," said Jim. "The district attorney, Doug Shepard, subpoenaed me and when I was called to testify he wanted me to identify the shooter. I pointed at Duane Harvey and said, 'That's your man.' Then Shepard showed me photographs of Mac after he was dead. Mac was almost unrecognizable. His face was swollen, black and blue, bruised real, real bad. He had suffered a way worse beating than any boxer I've ever seen. In my opinion, there's just no way any man's bare fists could have inflicted that much damage. Irwin had to have had a weapon. Later I heard a doctor had testified at the trial and said the beating Mac absorbed might very well have killed him if the bullet hadn't. I don't know about that, but the photographs showed Mac was beat to hell and back. Another thing that bothered me was I heard Harvey and Irwin, when they drove to Bend after the shooting, stopped to stash the derringer and Irwin's white turtleneck sweater in a juniper tree. That sure as hell proves Harvey was a coward and guilty of trying to distance himself from the weapon. Sure as hell does.

"When I testified, both Shepard and Bodie kept me on the straight and narrow. I never got a chance to say what happened; to tell my side of the story. All they let me answer was with a yes or no. Well, a yes or no doesn't always fit. Sometimes there are extenuating circumstances that need to be explained. But I was never allowed any latitude. It was strictly yes or no.

"I was stunned when the verdict came down for not guilty. Hell, I was in that parking lot. I know what went down. Duane Harvey was not threatened; no way was he threatened. He could have got the hell out of there at any time. In my opinion, Harvey was nothing but a lowlife. The son of a bitch got away with murder. He killed a man who was not, could not have, put up any resistance. What we had was an old fashioned fistfight in a parking lot, until Harvey showed up and pulled a gun, and then it was the Shootout at the O.K. Corral.

"What still bothers me is that Mac had the ability to be someone special. If he had lived he would be featured in the Rodeo Cowboy Hall of Fame; one of the best of the best. But Mac was a shooting star who flamed out too goddamn early."

PART FOUR

Crook County courthouse
(Oregonian *newspaper, February 3, 1965)*

The Trial

After Mac Griffith was pronounced dead, his body was taken to the Prineville Funeral Home. And although it was early in the investigation, the Prineville Police and the Crook County Sheriff's deputies had come to the conclusion a local man, Duane Claire Harvey, age 33, had been the shooter, and that at least one off-duty Oregon State Police trainee was somehow involved. An arrest warrant was issued for Harvey. He was taken into custody at 5:30 a.m. at his residence, a room at the Hacienda Motel in Prineville. The same day as the shooting, December 16, 1964, the *Bend Bulletin* newspaper reported, "Officers said Harvey apparently drove to Bend and returned prior to his arrest, but the reason for the trip was not clear. Harvey offered no resistance when he was arrested."

The newspaper went on to note an autopsy had been performed by Dr. George McGeary, the pathologist on the staff of St. Charles Memorial Hospital, Bend. He had concluded the cause of death was a massive hemorrhage, the result of a gunshot wound. Dr. McGeary was quoted, "The nature of the wound indicated the death weapon was apparently a .22 caliber pistol. The bullet entered the chest at the right side and lodged in the back. It was removed, but was disintegrated too much for positive identification."

Also reported was that Harvey had been arraigned in Prineville Justice Court before Justice Silas Taylor, and charged with first degree murder. The arraignment was continued for several hours while Harvey sought to secure counsel. Prineville attorney, James Bodie, was retained by Harvey. The arraignment hearing ended with Harvey lodged in the Crook County jail.

Tex King, Crook County sheriff, issued a press release stating, "The shooting was apparently the outgrowth of an altercation between three cowboys—Mac Griffith, Ronnie Raymond and Jim Bothum—and Larry Irwin, an Oregon State Police trainee, who was off duty at the time. How Harvey became involved is not clear at this time."

The day after the killing, with the autopsy completed, Mac Griffith's body was released and Jerry Sweeney, owner of Sweeney Funeral Home in Heppner, drove to Prineville through a blizzard and returned the body to Heppner. The funeral service was scheduled to be held at the Heppner First Christian Church, at 2 p.m. on Saturday.

Newspapers throughout the Northwest reported the shooting. Headlines broadcast, *"Top Rodeo Star, Mac Griffith Killed,"* and *"Prineville Row Fells Griffith,"* and *"Mac Griffith Shot to Death,"* and *"Mac Griffith, 1963 All-Around Champion, Victim of Gunshot,"* and *"Last Go-Round For Mac Griffith."*

Oregon State Police Superintendent, H. C. Maison, fired probationary State Police trainee, Larry Irwin, citing his involvement in the events that led to the shooting in the parking lot behind the Ochoco Inn. The other state police trainee, Ron Crawford, who left the scene before the fight and subsequent shooting, was suspended, then reinstated and sent from Prineville to Arlington.

In a *Bend Bulletin* newspaper article, Crook County Sheriff, Tex King was quoted as saying, "Jimmy Bothum, a bronc rider from Woodburn, and one of the men drinking with Mac Griffith in the Cinnabar Lounge prior to the shooting, told me he was standing beside Griffith when he was shot. According to Bothum, Duane Harvey drove his car into the parking lot during an altercation, walked to where a group of men was gathered and shot Mac Griffith.

"Bothum was treated at Pioneer Memorial Hospital for lacerations to his left arm and shoulder from an injury he suffered when he was knocked to the ground by Larry Irwin. Bothum was held in jail for a short time yesterday as a material witness, but posted $500 bond and was released. Sheriff Tex King accompanied him to the hospital for treatment of a shoulder injury."

The story concluded by noting, "The bullet taken from Griffith's body following the autopsy was taken last night by armed guard to the State Crime laboratory in Portland for complete analysis."

On Christmas Eve, the grand jury, comprised of four women and three men, was convened and listened to the evidence against Duane Harvey as presented by District Attorney Doug Shepard. They had the opportunity to question the eight witnesses who had been subpoenaed to appear, and they issued a true bill against Duane Harvey, but reduced the charge from first degree murder, which required proof of premeditation, to second degree murder. Jim Bodie asked that bail be set for his client. The Honorable Circuit Judge Robert H. Foley granted that request and set bail at $5,000. Bodie promptly posted a cashier's check and Harvey was released. It was announced the trial for Duane Harvey would be conducted within 30 to 40 days.

*****

As the prosecution and defense began preparing their cases, several storms slammed into Oregon, dumping a couple feet of snow. Then a Chinook wind roared in from out of the south. Warm winds licked at the snowdrifts. The sullen sky sagged lower, and torrential rains sluiced away at the deep snow. Fields became muddy bogs and cows walking fence lines made sucking sounds as their hooves were pulled from the holding mud. Everywhere the creeks and rivers and washes inflated with runoff and mud. It was the worst flooding in recorded history. Bend set a rainfall record for a 48-hour period when 3.55 inches was recorded. Giant boulders rolled off the steep hillsides northwest of Madras, closing the main link to Portland; the Santiam Highway was blocked by landsides near Blue Lake; the road over Ochoco Summit was washed out and Highway 97, to California, was under water and impassable. Central Oregon was isolated from the outside world.

*****

On December 26, 1964, the *Bend Bulletin* newspaper reported, "Duane Harvey, 33, Prineville, pleaded not guilty at his arraignment in circuit court to the charge of second degree murder.

"Harvey was first charged with murder in the first degree following the fatal shooting of Mac Griffith. The shooting followed a fracas in a parking lot at the rear of the Ochoco Inn building in downtown Prineville at 1:30 a.m.

"As the arraignment began, defense attorney Jim Bodie demurred to the indictment on the basis of the wording of the charge. District Attorney Douglas Shepard defended the wording of the indictment, and the attorneys clashed verbally."

*****

Crook County, situated in the geographic center of Oregon, was carved from the southern part of Wasco County and named after U.S. Army Major-General George Crook, who was credited with annihilating the population of local Indians during the Snake Indian Wars of the late 1860s. Crook County was twice reduced in size with the creation of Jefferson County in 1914, and Deschutes County in 1916. The final boundaries were set at nearly 3,000 square miles of rugged terrain.

In the early days, the imposing Cascade Mountain Range created a barrier to travel from the settled Willamette Valley, limiting migration to Central Oregon until the Santiam Wagon Road was completed in 1865. The Oregon Legislative Assembly established Prineville, the first major town in Central Oregon, as the county seat of Crook County on October 24, 1882. The town, named for the first merchant, Barney Prine, was founded in the heart of a broad valley, where winters linger late and the first frost comes early. The area became well-known for growing quality hay and cattle, and for the vast stands of ponderosa pine which were quickly being slashed off at the stump, brought to town and milled into high-grade lumber. By the 1960s, rusty wigwam burners stood hulking over the sawmills scattered around the town, the screened tops glowing a cheerful orange; burning sawdust and waste and pushing out brown smoke and white ash that hung in a perpetual smear over the town and valley. Death in Crook County was a common theme; out in the hills a horse went down, a bull gored a cowboy; in the woods a widow-maker fell, a saw slipped, a mistake was made; and in the mills, men lost fingers and toes and sometimes their lives.

The news of the day, as reported in the weekly local newspaper, the *Central Oregonian*, could vary from one man shooting another with his grandfather's 45-70 vintage buffalo gun, a black bear wandering into town and taking up residence in an apple tree, someone dying fighting a forest fire, a buckaroo struck by lightning, or joyriding teenagers killed when the driver lost control of an automobile. For the citizens of Crook County, their everyday lives proved death came quickly and often.

A ramshackle, one-story wooden courthouse, located at the corner of West 5th and Main Streets, was replaced in 1885 with a two-story wooden structure. Thirty years later the building was deemed unsafe. Voters approved a bond to build a stone and brick courthouse in the center of Prineville, which was completed in 1909, at a cost of nearly $78,000. This imposing building featured a grand clock tower designed to be viewed from all four directions.

It was in this historic courthouse, beneath the basalt rimrock outcroppings of the surrounding whiskey-colored countryside, where the Honorable Judge Robert H. Foley was called upon to preside over the trial of the *State of Oregon v. Duane Claire Harvey* on the charge of murder in the second degree. Promptly at 10 o'clock in the morning, on the first day of February, 1965, the courtroom doors were closed. Disappointed groans were audible from those denied admittance and who remained standing in the hallway and on the wide staircase.

The mood in the courtroom quickly became somber and so hushed that the sounds of individuals' breathing became audible. The attorneys, dressed professionally in suits and ties and armed with files of papers, pens and white legal pads, sat at two tables. They looked every bit as fidgety and eager to begin the proceedings as prizefighters awaiting the bell. The jurors' faces conveyed a look of sincerity and eagerness, as if they were willing to forget whatever they might have heard about the case, and give the accused his day in court. The defendant, Duane Harvey, nervously squirmed in his chair, and glanced over his left shoulder, but instead of seeing individuals he might know, he saw only a wispy blur of unrecognizable faces.

Judge Foley entered the room with a rush, black robe swishing, and stepped to his bench, an elevated platform backlit by a bank of tall windows. He took his seat in a wooden swivel chair, checking to make sure it swiveled to his liking, and then he leaned back.

Judge Foley had been on the bench for years, was about to retire, and looked exactly like a judge is supposed to look: dignified, white-haired, amiable, and yet he was every bit a no-nonsense man who required strict adherence to the rules of courtroom etiquette. He was a stickler for following the exact letter of the law. He demanded respect, and yet he practiced informality, taking copious notes and occasionally resting his eyes until it appeared he might have actually dozed off. Nor was Judge Foley above occasionally removing his pocketknife from a trouser pocket beneath his venerable black robe to clean his fingernails, if he deemed they needed cleaning.

Judge Foley knew the Oregon Revised Statutes inside and out, and could make a legal ruling on some minor point of law on the spur of the moment. His decisions were seldom overturned by a higher court. For the most part, Judge Foley went about the business of being a judge with what seemed to be casual indifference, allowing the attorneys a lot of rope while maintaining a firm grip on the end of that rope. The court reporter was seated in front of the judge's stand, and the witness chair was to the left of the judge. The prosecution and defense tables were arranged nearly side-by-side, facing the stand. The jury was seated in two solemn rows of six in the corner of the room nearest the witness stand. All this was surrounded by an ornately rugged wooden railing, the barrier behind which the audience was seated in rows of pews like might be found in a church.

As jury selection got underway, the courtroom was filled to capacity with the overflow standing along the back wall. Onlookers witnessed the district attorney, Doug Shepard, and the defense attorney, Jim Bodie, sparring like a couple of aggressive and spirited barnyard roosters attempting to establish territorial rights and dominance. They clashed frequently as they exercised peremptory challenges and had potential jurors dismissed for cause. The *Bend Bulletin* newspaper noted, "Judge Robert H. Foley is trying the case. The courtroom was filled. Among the persons in the courtroom were the defendant's mother, Mrs. Florence Wilcox, employed as a cook in Potlatch, Idaho, and his brother-in-law and sister, Mr. and Mrs. Rex Gustavson, and their son, Dennis, from Portland."

The jury that was eventually seated included nine women and three men: Coy Short, a dairy store owner; Beryl Landers, housewife; Roxie Shell, housewife; Gladys Bowman, housewife; Lucille Streetman, housewife; Rose Gregson, housewife; Gertrude Bengston, housewife; Charles Kelmer, teacher; Dick Hoppes, laundry owner; George Oglesby, retired; Geneva Berry, appliance store co-owner; Violet Pinkard, bank clerk; and Richard Helms, millworker, was named as alternate.

*****

The trial of Duane Harvey began the morning of February 2, 1965. A low-lying smoky fog, the color and texture of skim milk, hung tight to the ground, but would soon burn off to reveal a few fluffy white clouds scudding across a wide expanse of vivid blue sky. The air was cold. Snow remained in patches. The barometer was on the rise.

District Attorney Doug Shepard, began the proceedings in the courtroom with his opening statement in which he declared the prosecution would prove beyond a reasonable doubt that Duane Harvey killed Mac Griffith, and that his motive was jealousy and revenge. For the defense, Jim Bodie, asserted his client acted in self-defense, to protect his life and that of another.

The prosecution began presenting its case by calling Oregon State Police trainee Ronald E. Crawford to the stand. Crawford had driven down from Arlington, where he had been transferred. He was wearing his blue Oregon State Police uniform, and gave the appearance he was definitely official and trustworthy. He sat erect in the witness chair and testified that he had accompanied Jerry Hubbard and Larry Irwin to the Cinnabar Lounge at about 10 p.m. on December 15, 1964.

"Tell me what happened," requested Shepard.

"We sat at a table and ordered dinner," said Crawford. "After about an hour of general conversation we noticed some commotion at the bar between Mr. Griffith, Mr. Raymond and one other man. A stool and a drink were thrown. It was over fast. The bartender quieted everyone down. Then Mr. Irwin and Mr. Griffith argued. I don't know what about. Mr. Hubbard and I were able to diffuse that situation and Mr. Griffith returned to the bar. Mr. Hubbard and I decided to leave. Mr. Irwin stated he wanted to stay. We walked to my place, six blocks away, and got my car so I could take Mr. Hubbard back to Bend. We stopped at the Cinnabar to see if Mr. Irwin had changed his mind about going home.

"When we got in the bar we found everyone standing up, grouped around Mr. Irwin. It appeared as if something was going on. We again asked Mr. Irwin if he wanted to leave. He replied he wished to stay. Mr. Hubbard and I walked out and drove to the Brownfield Café for coffee. While we were drinking coffee, we saw an ambulance go by. We got up and followed, arriving at the Ochoco Inn parking lot in time to see Mr. Griffith being loaded into the ambulance. We reported the matter to the city police, and then headed to Bend."

The second witness, Jerry Hubbard, variety store manager in Bend, a former U. S. Marine and the roommate of Larry Irwin, gave virtually the same testimony as Crawford. When he concluded his remarks, Doug Shepard asked him, "Did you feel the altercations you witnessed in the bar that night warranted you contacting the city police or sheriff's office?"

"No, sir," responded Hubbard.

"One more question," said Shepard. "As you left the Cinnabar to go have a cup of coffee, did you see anything out of the ordinary?"

"No, sir," responded Hubbard. "The parking lot was empty, except for a few cars parked here and there. It was empty of people. We didn't notice anyone."

Bodie shook his head, letting Judge Foley know he had no questions to ask of the witness, and Jerry Hubbard stepped down.

*****

"I call Patricia Elaine Leonard," announced Shepard, and a minute later Pat Leonard, the bartender and night manager of the Cinnabar Lounge, was escorted to the stand. She was conservatively dressed and very nice-looking. Heads turned to follow her as she made her way to the witness stand. After being sworn in, she took a seat in the witness chair, deliberately crossing one leg over the other, smoothing her skirt and nervously folding her hands and placing them on her lap. She looked toward Shepard who was busy at his table. She waited as he pushed away a few papers in front of him and stood. He asked Pat to state her full name, spell it, state her address and tell what her position was at the Cinnabar Lounge. She answered each of his questions.

"What time did you come to work on the evening of December 15, 1964?" asked Shepard, his back muscles stiffening slightly.

"About 6 p.m.," answered Pat.

"And can you tell me the names of the customers in the bar that evening?"

"I can tell you their names, what they were drinking and how much I served them," said Pat proudly.

"Objection," bellowed Bodie.

Judge Foley stirred. He turned slowly in his swivel chair, looked benignly out over his courtroom and loudly proclaimed, "Sustained." Turning to Pat he directed her, "Answer the question that is asked. Please refrain from making impulsive, off-the-cuff remarks. Answer the question as simply as possible."

Pat named her customers. Shepard then asked Pat if she knew Mac Griffith. She said she did. Shepard asked if she knew Duane Harvey. Again Pat replied in the affirmative.

"Did you notice any conflict between Griffith and Harvey?" asked Shepard.

"Not really," said Pat. "But Griffith started to get pretty loud. He was insulting me, and then paying me compliments. Harvey suggested I siwash Griffith."

Shepard looked confused and asked, "Siwash, what does that mean?"

"Kick him out of the bar," said Pat. She leaned forward slightly. "That made me mad because I had known Griffith for a long time, had served him on many occasions, and knew Griffith was just kidding around."

"And then what happened?" prompted Shepard.

"Griffith started saying things derogatory about state cops," said Pat. "He knew Irwin and Crawford worked for the state police."

"What did he say?" asked Shepard.

Bodie started to stand. He had one hand raised to object, thought better of it and sat down in his chair.

"I remember him saying, 'There's only one thing I do better than ride, and that's fight,'" said Pat. "I went up to Griffith and asked him why he had to pick on a state cop. He just grinned. Then Irwin invited Griffith to his table, and Griffith got up saying, 'Ain't no coyote in me,' and everything seemed fine. After a few minutes Griffith returned to the bar and Harvey sat down at the table with Irwin. Everything seemed fine and then an argument of some kind broke out. Harvey stood, lifted a chair over his shoulder. I yelled at him to put it down, but instead he threw the chair and it hit Bob Clark in the face. Ronnie Raymond put his hand on Harvey and said, 'Leave him alone. He's an old man.'

"And then Irwin was pushing someone and I tried to stop them. Ronnie lifted me up and set me out of the way. Irwin took a swing at Ronnie and they fell on the floor. Ronnie was on top. Don Chase picked Ronnie up and set him in a chair, kept him there. Griffith had hold of Irwin by the arms, and when he turned him loose he said, 'You're not going to fight any more.'

"Irwin turned away, and as he passed Griffith, he said, 'Let's go finish this thing,' or something to that effect. Mac took off his coat, folded it up and laid it over the back of a chair. Irwin went to the door and waited. Mac told one of his friends, 'I'm going outside to teach a cop a lesson.' They went out the door together.

"Pretty soon everyone decided to go out and watch the fight. As soon as they were out the door, I locked up, cleared the till, took the money to the hotel desk and it was put in the safe. Then I got busy cleaning up.

"Someone started banging on the back door. It was Ronnie Raymond. I let him in. He said Mac had been shot. I called for the ambulance and ran to the parking lot. Mary Edgerly was there. Mac Griffith was lying on his side, unconscious, just moaning. He rolled over, then rolled back on his side and didn't moan any more. There was blood all over his face, even in his ears. I tried to find out where he was hurt. Then the police and ambulance came and took him away."

Again Shepard returned to his table and took a few moments rearranging his notes. He quietly whispered something to his co-counsel, Fred Robinson. After Robinson answered, Shepard walked to the stand, and when he was only a few feet from Pat Leonard, he fired a question at her, asking, "Isn't it true you have an ongoing relationship with Mr. Harvey, and that Mr. Harvey was jealous of the attention Mac Griffith was paying to you?"

Jim Bodie was on his feet, objecting, and Judge Foley asked Shepard where he was going with this line of questioning. Shepard replied, "I intend to use the testimony of this witness to prove malice and motive on the part of the defendant."

Judge Foley gave forth an exaggerated sigh and excused the jury while details of the *relationship* between Duane Harvey and Pat Leonard could be recounted and explored. The judge asked Pat about how many dates she and Mr. Harvey had gone on. Pat stated they had had approximately a dozen dates.

"Were these romantic dates?" asked Judge Foley.

"Not really," said Pat, and she explained that on one *date* she had accompanied Harvey, and his cousin, Bill Metcalf, to the 86 Corral, a bar in Redmond. Pat said she offered to read Metcalf's palm, and Harvey became extremely agitated.

"Why were you going to read his palm? Are you a psychic?" asked Judge Foley.

"Heavens no," responded Pat. "It was just for kicks."

Judge Foley glanced in the direction of Shepard, and then Bodie. He made his ruling, sustaining Bodie's objection and informing the district attorney he was not allowed to introduce any testimony regarding any *dates* between Pat and Harvey because the connection was "too remote to be of any use in establishing malice or motive."

On cross-examination, Bodie asked the witness, "Were you aware that Mac Griffith had a reputation as a mean man, a barroom brawler?"

"Yes sir, but..." said Pat.

Bodie stopped Pat from saying any more by raising his right hand and strutting to the center of the room. He said, "Please answer the question with a simple yes or no, Mrs. Leonard." He glared at her and turned away, leisurely passing in front of the jury so they were forced to look at him. Bodie wheeled toward the witness and asked, "So you knew of Mac Griffith's reputation as a brawler, and you were also probably aware that he has gotten in any number of fights and has sent his opponents to the hospital in serious condition? Is that correct, Mrs. Leonard? Yes, or no?"

Pat considered the question carefully, and seemed to decide on an answer. She said, "Yes." It was obvious she had more she wanted to add, but Bodie never allowed her the opportunity to explain herself.

Bodie turned all of his attention to the witness and demanded to know, "And why was it that you did not cut Mr. Griffith off sooner? Were you afraid if you cut him off, and did not serve him more alcohol, he would become even more aggressive and violent?"

"With Mac it was hard to tell," Pat began to explain. "He was well-coordinated and it was hard...."

Again Bodie stopped her. "A simple yes or no will suffice, Mrs. Leonard."

Pat hesitated and grudgingly responded, "Yes."

*****

In answer to the bailiff's baritone voice calling his name, a wiry man who moved with the grace and quickness of a cougar on the prowl, took the stand. He had a fresh haircut, and was well-dressed in gray slacks, white shirt with an open collar and a cream-colored, knee-length duster jacket. As he was being sworn in he seemed confident and relaxed; once seated he was asked to state his name. He said, "Larry Olen Irwin." His voice oozed practiced charm.

"What can you tell me about the night in question, December 15, 1964?" asked Fred Robinson, who was handling the questioning of this witness for the State.

"What do you want to know?" said Irwin, flashing a grin.

"What did you witness when you were in the bar?" asked Robinson.

Irwin claimed to have witnessed Mac Griffith and another fellow he didn't know, sparring in the bar. He recalled, "Mr. Griffith was loud and boastful, challenging all of us in the bar to engage him in a fistfight. At one point Mr. Griffith grabbed the bartender around the waist and wouldn't let her go. He finally did, and then he joined our table. We bought each other a round. We seemed to be getting along."

"Tell this court about the fight in the bar," said Robinson.

"There was a group of men sitting at our table," said Irwin. "One of them made a comment to me, saying, 'I hear you're a state cop. If you caught John Hudspeth speeding would you give him a ticket?' And my reply was, 'Hell, yes, if he deserved it, I'd write him up.' Mr. Hudspeth, who was sitting at the table, took offense. He said he'd be damned if he'd take a ticket from me. He jumped up. Then Mr. Griffith was there, standing over me. I was seated. He tried to intimidate me, and told me to shut my mouth and not pick on an old man. He said if I was looking for trouble, he would give me all the trouble I wanted."

"Do you think he was trying to push you into a fistfight?" asked Robinson.

"Yes I do," responded Irwin. "I tried to diffuse the situation by telling Mr. Hudspeth there was no reason for him to be offended. The question was silly, but I had answered it to the best of my ability. I didn't care who it was, or how rich he was, or how many mills he owned, if he deserved a ticket, I'd sure as hell write him up. But rather than soothe the situation, my comment seemed to inflame the hostilities. Ronnie Raymond came over with a drink in his hand. He dropped one shoulder and moved toward me like he was going to hit me. I was still seated, but I threw a punch that caught him in the solar plexus. He fell backward against the bar and we tumbled onto the floor. Mr. Raymond was on top."

"And then what happened?" prompted Robinson.

"The defendant, Mr. Harvey, and others broke it up," said Irwin. "Mr. Griffith was standing behind me. He said, 'If you've got trouble with Raymond, you'll have to come through me.' I ignored him, tried to talk to Mr. Hudspeth and explain things, but he turned away. Mr. Griffith crowded me, and it was at that point I suggested to Mr. Griffith we go outside, by ourselves, and settle our differences. He agreed.

"But before any of that happened, earlier when I was sitting in the Rustler's Roost, adjacent to the bar with Mr. Crawford and Mr. Hubbard, a Prineville policeman who I recognized as Jim Jones, came in and I told him it appeared the bar was getting a little rowdy. Mr. Jones said there was nothing he could do about the situation, that the management of the bar didn't seem to care if there was fighting or not. He pointed out Mr. Griffith, and went on to relate he had fought two loggers in Prineville and put them both in the hospital. He warned me about Mr. Griffith, said he was a professional fighter and generally a bad egg."

Bodie was listening intently to this testimony. There was a slight trace of a smile tugging at the corners of his lips, but his brow was furrowed as he pondered why Robinson was allowing Irwin to ramble and introduce testimony which was advantageous to the defense. It seemed as though the prosecution was playing into the hands of the defense, and Bodie searched his mind for any possible gambit on the part of the prosecution, found none, and began to relax.

In an effort to get Irwin back on track, Fred Robinson said, "Tell me about the fight you were involved in with Mr. Griffith."

"Mr. Griffith and I went outside," said Irwin. "I was hoping when I got him away from his friends he would be less confrontational. I had absolutely no intention of fighting him. In the bar, there had been several incidents where Mr. Griffith had appeared to be reasonable. I was hoping he would be rational, and that we could talk things out without having to resort to fighting. But on the way, as we drew near the parking lot—my right hand was resting on Mr. Griffith's left shoulder—he suddenly shifted his weight and swung on me. I felt two stiff jolts and my head snapped back. At that point I was forced to take retaliatory action. I hit him twice. He went down."

A surprised murmur of disbelief rustled through the packed courtroom. Judge Foley banged his gavel, admonished the audience and threatened to clear the courtroom. He addressed the witness, instructing Irwin to continue.

"I got Mr. Griffith on the ground, pinned his arms to his sides with my legs and told him to give up," said Irwin smugly. "But he persisted, refusing to give up. I grabbed the back of his head and hit him three times."

"How hard did you hit him?" asked Robinson.

"As hard as I could from a sitting position," said Irwin.

"Was he unconscious?" asked Robinson.

"I don't know. He just laid there and took it," said Irwin. "I thought maybe he was playing possum. From the time Mr. Griffith first hit me, my vision was blurred and my knees were wobbly."

"What happened next?"

"I was starting to get up when the other cowboys showed up; Ronnie Raymond and Jimmy Bothum."

Judge Foley stopped taking notes as he had been doing, laid his pencil aside and interrupted the proceedings at that tense moment in Irwin's testimony to declare noon recess. The audience expelled a sigh seemingly as one, and then silently filed from the courtroom.

After the noon recess, Irwin returned to the stand and Robinson asked him why he continued to strike Griffith when it appeared Griffith was unable to fight back. Irwin replied, "I wanted to put him away because I was expecting the other cowboys to show up and jump me. But I couldn't seem to knock out Mr. Griffith."

"You stated you had stopped fighting and were getting to your feet when two cowboys showed up; Ronnie Raymond and Jim Bothum," said Robinson.

"Correct," said Irwin. "Those two cowboys came up on me fast, from my blind side. Mr. Bothum got to me first and I hit him. He fell and I ran ten or twelve steps across the parking lot. By then Mr. Griffith was on his feet, crouching in his fighter's stance. I ran to where there was a row of parking meters, spun around one and kicked out, trying to keep the three cowboys away from me. I was still dizzy and shaky. I realized I was not going to get away, and I couldn't fight any more. I figured my best chance was to get to the bar door and try and get inside. I ran in that direction, but someone jumped high on my back, driving me down, and I fell, smashing my head into the pavement. I saw legs standing over me. I don't know how many cowboys were there. Someone kicked at my head, but I managed to twist and the blow landed on my arm. Then I was kicked in the ribs. They kept hitting and kicking me. There are periods where I don't remember. I was only half conscious when I realized someone was yelling to break it up. Duane Harvey was lifting me off the pavement."

"And Mr. Harvey got you to his car," said Robinson.

"That's right," acknowledged Irwin. "We drove to his motel room where he helped clean me up. It was his suggestion I take off my bloody white sweater. He gave me another. He said I needed to go to the hospital, but said the cowboys would be waiting for us at the hospital in Prineville, and he suggested we drive to Bend. On the way there he stopped his car, got out, and walked off the road, taking my bloody sweater with him. He either put it up in a tree or hid it behind a tree. I didn't question him.

"Did he show you a gun?" asked Robinson.

"Not at that point. But he confided that he had fired a weapon to stop the fight," said Irwin.

"Continue," directed Robinson.

"Mr. Harvey drove me to the Bend hospital, where the cuts in my mouth and on my face were sewn up, and I was treated for a rib separation. I had also lost some teeth."

"And what did you tell the doctor was the cause of your injuries?" asked Robinison.

"I told the doctor I had slipped on the ice and bumped my head."

"And why did you say that?"

"I thought it would reflect poorly on the Oregon State Police to have an officer involved in a fistfight," explained Irwin. "After they finished sewing me up at the hospital, Mr. Harvey drove me to my apartment. I immediately called my State Police sergeant at home, woke him up and explained the facts of the incident to him and admitted my involvement."

"I have no further questions of this witness," stated Robinson.

Bodie was momentarily caught off guard. His chair was sitting skewed to one side, and his left arm was draped over the back of the chair. He raked the fingers on his right hand through his receding hairline, and pushed his glasses up the bridge of his nose. He rose to his feet and began his cross-examination with a lengthy statement, rambling on about how Prineville was known as the *Cowboy Capital of the World*, that the town had become a popular layover for cowboys on the rodeo circuit, and that the Cinnabar Lounge was a favorite watering hole for these cowboys. He asked Irwin if he was aware of Griffith's reputation as a brawler and Irwin responded he was well aware of Griffith's reputation. Bodie then asked Irwin if he was afraid for his personal safety and well-being when the two cowboys, Raymond and Bothum, showed up in the parking lot. Irwin changed his previous statement slightly, saying, "When the two cowboys showed up I got up off Griffith and started backpedaling. But they kept coming at me."

"Was Mac Griffith a good fighter?" asked Bodie.

Irwin shifted in the witness chair; sat a little straighter and his chest swelled as he responded, "I've been hit by some good punchers, but Mr. Griffith hit me as hard as I've ever been hit."

Bodie drew a sudden breath, as if in surprise at Irwin's statement, and then guiding the witness he stated, "You got up and ran."

"Yes I did," said Irwin. "As I was getting up I saw Mr. Griffith get up, too. He was grinning like a crazy man. He dropped into a fighting crouch. I was tired. I couldn't go no more. I was played out. Three against one isn't a fair fight."

"You say Griffith got into a fighting stance," said Bodie. "Would you please step down from the witness stand and demonstrate that stance."

Larry Irwin stepped down. He crouched, hands up protecting himself, bobbing and weaving like a boxer in the ring. He said, "He was like this, was ready to keep fighting."

"You can retake your seat," advised Bodie. After Irwin was seated in the witness chair, Bodie continued, directing the witness, "Now tell me about what happened after you tried to get away, when Raymond tackled you."

"I got tackled from behind and didn't know if there was one man, or three, on top of me," said Irwin. "I was trying to protect my head but someone kicked me in the ribs and I brought my hands down. When I did, I got kicked in the face. My mouth got cut, my lip was split and I lost some teeth."

"Did you yell for help?" prompted Bodie. The pattern of Bodie's questioning was becoming obvious. He had already established the cowboys posed a serious danger and now he was trying to elicit specific testimony verifying that Larry Irwin felt he was in imminent danger of losing his life.

"Hell yes," responded Irwin.

"What did you say? Did you say, "Help! Help! They're killing me!"

"That's what I said."

"Tell me the exact words you shouted."

"Help! Help! They're killing me!" repeated Irwin.

"And you thought you were going to die?" said Bodie. "You thought those cowboy thugs were going to use their boots and kick you to death, didn't you?"

"Yes, I thought they were going to kill me," said Irwin. "I passed out."

"And what happened when you woke up? Was Duane Harvey there helping you?"

"Yes he was. He helped me to his car. He drove me to his motel room. I was covered with blood and dirt. He cleaned me up the best he could, and then we took off for the hospital in Bend."

"Is this the sweater you were wearing that night?" asked Bodie, holding up a white sweater stained with splotches of red.

"Yes, that's my sweater," testified Irwin. "Mr. Harvey drove me to the hospital in Bend, and on the way we stopped in the middle of nowhere. There were no lights around. Mr. Harvey said he was scared, said he might be in trouble, and confided that during the fight, 'I had to shoot at one of the cowboys and I might have winged him.'"

Irwin now changed his previous statement in which he said Harvey had not shown him the weapon. This time Irwin testified, "He showed me a derringer pistol, and said he had warned the cowboys he would use it if they didn't stop fighting. They charged him, he said, and he had no recourse but to fire. Harvey took the pistol, and my bloody sweater, hiked a little ways from the road and put them in a juniper tree.

"After that we drove straight to the hospital. The doctor had to stitch up my face, and inside my mouth, and told me I would have to see a dentist about my missing teeth. He thought I might have a concussion. Mr. Harvey drove me to the apartment I share with my roommate, Jerry Hubbard. Mr. Harvey then departed for Prineville."

Again Irwin changed his previous testimony, saying, "After he was gone, Mr. Hubbard, my roommate, called from Prineville, told me what had happened, that Mr. Griffith was dead. I immediately reported the matter to my sergeant, calling him at his home and informing him of the events of the evening."

"Was Griffith a big man? Was he a formidable opponent?" asked Bodie.

"Yes he was," said Irwin. "He was big and he was strong. He knew how to fight too. In the bar that night I was told by Prineville officer, Mr. Jones, that Mr. Griffith had been a professional boxer, had had eight professional fights and won all eight by knockout. Mr. Jones informed me he had been on duty the night Mr. Griffith sent two loggers to the hospital. He warned me that Mr. Griffith was nobody to mess with."

"And you believed him?" said Bodie.

"Yes," replied Irwin. "Mr. Griffith was much stronger than I am. I do believe, if he and his two buddies had had their way that night, they might very well have killed me because I was a state policeman."

"One last question, Mr. Irwin," said Bodie. "In your opinion, at any time during the evening, did you observe Mr. Harvey acting in an aggressive manner?"

"Quite the contrary," said Irwin. "I never witnessed Mr. Harvey start any trouble. In fact, in every instance, he was more of a peacemaker."

During Larry Irwin's prolonged testimony—even though it was obvious Bodie was extracting information absolutely crucial to the defense and very damaging to the prosecution— neither Shepard nor Robinson ever launched a single objection. The two men continued to sit quietly at their table, side by side, as mesmerize by Bodie's skillful manipulation of the witness as everyone else in the courtroom appeared to be. Bodie triumphantly informed the judge he had no further questions.

The *Oregonian,* a Portland newspaper that not only sent a reporter to cover the trial, but also a sketch artist, stated in a front page feature, "This trial has become this cow town's biggest drawing card since last year's rodeo. An hour before the trial began, the big courtroom on the second floor of the old Crook County Courthouse was jammed to the walls with spectators, most of them ranchers, cattlemen and curious townsfolk ... many of the men present wore cowboy hats, blue jeans and boots. An aura of the Old West was perceivable."

*****

On the second day of the trial, Ronnie Raymond was summoned to the stand. He was handsome and self-confident, wearing a western shirt with pearl snaps, and when asked to state his occupation he proudly answered, "Rodeo rider."

"When you were in the bar you were involved in an altercation. Can you tell me about that altercation?" asked Shepard.

Raymond replied, "The state cop ..."

"Are you referring to the Oregon State Police trainee, Larry Irwin?" asked Shepard.

Raymond nodded, said, "Yeah, Larry Irwin, the state cop. Irwin jumped me when I went over to see why John Hudspeth was upset. I took Irwin to the ground and it was over before it began. It was nothing."

Shepard changed his line of questioning, asking Raymond why he had chased Irwin and tackled him in the parking lot. Raymond responded, "I wanted to ask him why he kept hitting Mac after he was already on the ground."

"You chased him down and tackled him, did you not?" asked Shepard.

"Not exactly," drawled Raymond. "I grabbed his arm and he more or less fell to the ground in front of me." The crowd snickered and Judge Foley looked up in a reprimanding manner. As soon as the room quieted, he instructed Shepard to carry on, and he returned to writing in his notebook.

"Did you hit him?" asked Shepard.

"He didn't answer me when I asked him why he kept hitting Mac," said Raymond. "He swung on me and I popped him a few times. Then Jimmy, Jim Bothum, pulled me off and said Mac had been shot and that I was next, something like that. I looked up and Harvey was standing there with a chrome-plated pistol pointed at me, and I jumped up, ran into the hotel and called for an ambulance."

Bodie, in his cross-examination of Raymond, asked how many drinks Raymond had consumed prior to the fight in the parking lot. Raymond thought he had maybe had a couple, and maintained he was sober the entire evening.

"Even when Irwin was running away, you chased him down. Did you do that to protect Griffith?" asked Bodie.

"Irwin had hit me once in the bar. Why should he have the right to hit me, and I don't have the right to hit him?" asked Raymond.

"I will ask the questions here," stated Bodie. "Mr. Irwin had hit you earlier, back inside the bar. Did you go after him because he had hit you earlier?"

"No. I already said I wanted to find out what he done to Mac," said Raymond. "I figured he had to have dry-gulched him."

"Dry-gulched," repeated Bodie.

"I figured Irwin jumped Mac, or hit him with something," said Raymond.

"And did you ask him?"

"He didn't answer," said Raymond.

Bodie started to walk away, and then turned and asked, "Are you tough?"

Raymond grinned and shrugged his shoulders. "I suppose. You gotta to be tough if you're gonna be a cowboy."

"Were you tougher than Mac Griffith?"

"We never fought," said Raymond.

Bodie had reached the defense table. He asked, "And why is that?"

Raymond's grin widened. "I may be a cowboy, but I ain't stupid."

The crowd understood the implication; that Raymond recognized Griffith would whip him in a fight, and although the room remained silent, most folks were smiling. Bodie rapped the knuckles of one hand against the wood for added emphasis and told the judge he was finished with the witness.

*****

155

James "Jimmy" Franklin Bothum was called to the stand. He entered the courtroom wearing his black cowboy hat and Shepard asked him to remove it before he was sworn in. Bothum took his seat in the witness chair, sitting as straight as a metal-T fence post, placing the hat casually on one knee. Shepard asked Bothum to tell what he observed when he entered the parking lot on the morning of December 16, 1964. Bothum said his first reaction was shock at seeing Mac Griffith on the ground. He said, "I didn't think anyone could knock Griffith down."

"And then what did you observe concerning Mr. Griffith?" asked Shepard.

"He got to his feet. He said he could fight. But he couldn't," said Bothum. "He was out of it."

Bothum went on to relate the details as Ronnie Raymond chased Larry Irwin around the parking lot, ending when Raymond tackled Irwin. He added, "Harvey shot Mac Griffith and he threatened me."

On cross-examination Bodie kept a tight rein on Bothum, allowing him very little latitude in his responses. Bothum became frustrated and red in the face. Each time he tried to explain himself, Bodie cut him off. And then Bodie accused Bothum of being a barroom brawler, placing him into the same category as Ronnie Raymond and Mac Griffith.

"You cowboys came to town looking for trouble, didn't you?" asked Bodie.

"No, We were just having a friendly drink and...."

Bodie interrupted, stating, "You were looking for someone to fight." Bothum started to answer, but Bodie, once again, cut him off. "That was a statement, Mr. Bothum, not a question," said Bodie arrogantly. "You need not try and answer a statement, Mr. Bothum."

It was obvious Bothum was like a race horse wanting to run, but not being allowed his head. What Bothum wanted to tell the jury was that after the fight, Griffith was hurt, hurt real bad, and was in no condition to fight anyone. In fact, Griffith was draped over Bothum's shoulders when Harvey suddenly produced a weapon, and without provocation, fired that weapon. He wanted to say a lot of things, but the legal system, and the power and control exerted by Bodie in the courtroom, kept him from saying any of those things. And Shepard, lacking experience, failed to read this witness and devise well constructed questions to draw forth testimony to bring out the truth.

*****

Mary Edgerly, former wife of Duane Harvey, was called to testify. As she raised her right hand and swore to tell the truth, the whole truth, and nothing but the truth, she seemed reticent, nervous, timid, shy and fragile. Her perfume gave an overpoweringly sweet smell of warm honeysuckle, and her voice, momentarily audible, quickly faded to little more than an earnest whisper, like the soft hiss of a radio signal lost to distance. Judge Foley repeatedly admonished her, asking her to speak louder. She gave the address of her current residence as "Paul's Trailer Court," and said she was unemployed. When asked if she had been married to Duane Harvey, she replied they were married in 1955. The marriage had lasted a little over two years, and during that time her husband, who was in the Air Force, was stationed overseas. She had only seen him a few times, when he was able to arrange leave. Throughout her testimony, Mary was constantly rebuked by Judge Foley, as well as both attorneys, for speaking too softly, and directed to repeat her testimony.

Shepard began his questioning of the witness by asking Mary to describe her ongoing relationship with Duane Harvey. She categorized it as "friendly."

"How many times have you seen Mr. Harvey since the night of the shooting?" asked Shepard.

Mary thought for a moment while glancing warily around the courtroom as if searching for some possible threat, and answered, "He has come to visit me on two occasions, and I have gone to the garage where he is employed three times."

Shepard waited for Mary—she was nervously wringing a white handkerchief in her hands—and asked, "Have you dated Mr. Harvey recently?"

"He asked me out, but I didn't go," said Mary.

"Duane Harvey cares about you, doesn't he?" asked Shepard.

Bodie strenuously objected, barking that the question required the witness to make a supposition. Judge Foley readjusted his glasses, cleared his throat and promptly sustained the objection.

"Had you met Mac Griffith before the night of December 15, 1964?" asked Shepard.

"No," said Mary softly.

"You were friendly with him. You danced with him."

"Yes," said Mary.

"How did Mr. Harvey react to you dancing with Mr. Griffith?"

"I didn't pay any attention."

"Why did you quit dancing with Mr. Griffith?" asked Shepard.

"He became vulgar."

"In what way did he become vulgar?" asked Shepard.

"He kept saying things...." Mary's voice trailed off and Shepard asked her to repeat what she had said in a louder voice. She was embarrassed, but replied, "He said, 'Let me rear up on you.'"

"At that point did you leave the Cinnabar?" asked Shepard.

"Yes," said Mary.

"Tell me, in your own words, what happened," said Shepard.

"I went outside with Lee Rhoden and Don Chase," said Mary. "We got in Don's car. I was between the two men. They were going to drive me home. We were starting to leave the parking lot when we saw a man running and another man chasing him. One man spun around a parking meter, and the other man jumped on his back and drove him to the ground."

"The man running, was he moving fast?" asked Shepard.

"Yes. He was trying to get away," said Mary.

"Did you notice anything before you saw the man running, and another man chasing him? Did you hear a gunshot?" asked Shepard.

"No," said Mary. "The car motor and heater were running. We were talking. I never saw anything, never heard anything."

"And then what happened?" prompted Shepard.

"Don started to drive, and Duane Harvey's car was blocking our way. He had pulled into the entrance to the parking lot, and was standing in front of his car. Griffith was on the ground in front of the car, maybe 30 feet away. I wanted to get out to see if I could help him, but Don and Lee wouldn't let me. They said they didn't want to get involved." Mary faltered for a moment, and then resumed her testimony. "Don drove to the front of the Ochoco Inn, and they stopped and let me out. I ran around the building to the parking lot and tried my best to get Mac on his feet, but he was hurt and he was bleeding. I was the only one there, and then others came."

"You stayed with him until the ambulance got there, right?" asked Shepard.

"Yes I did," said Mary. She deliberately opened the dainty handkerchief she had twisted into a sweaty rope, revealing a mass of wrinkled material, and used the handkerchief to dab at the corner of her eyes as she resolutely waited for the next question.

"And what did Mr. Griffith say? Was he responsive in any way?" asked Shepard.

"He moaned a few times. And he tried to roll over. But mostly he just laid there on the pavement and didn't move," said Mary.

During cross-examination, Bodie asked, "Did you see a gun in the hand of Mr. Harvey?"

"No. I never saw a gun," said Mary.

"At any time did you, or your two male companions, make any effort to stop the fight?" asked Bodie.

"No, we did not," said Mary.

"You did not make any effort to come to the aid of the Oregon State policeman, Larry Irwin, who was on the ground and being severely beaten?" asked Bodie.

"No," said Mary. She sniffled and used the kerchief to dab at her nose.

Bodie asked Mary to repeat her last statement. She again responded, "No."

*****

Don Chase, owner of Hay Creek Ranch located near Madras, took the witness stand dressed in a checkered shirt, blue work jeans and well-worn cowboy boots. His memory of the events he witnessed in the parking lot conflicted sharply with the testimony of Mary Edgerly. He related, "I saw the whole thing. Raymond and Bothum came upon where Mac Griffith and Larry Irwin were fighting. Duane Harvey joined the group, and then Irwin hit Bothum. Bothum went down. Griffith and Raymond started chasing Irwin toward the parking meters. They were sparring as they ran. When they got to the parking meters Irwin spun around, flailing with his feet, trying to keep the cowboys away from him. Then he took off running. Raymond chased him and caught him. By that time, Griffith was walking away from where Raymond and Irwin were fighting. I turned my head to respond to something Lee had said, and when I looked back, Griffith was making his way toward where Harvey was standing and his face was all bloody, his shirt was torn and he was walking bent over like he was hurt. When Griffith was 10 or 12 feet from Harvey, he collapsed onto the ground."

"Did you hear a shot?" asked Shepard.

"Lee and Mary were talking, the motor was running. I didn't hear nothin' that sounded like a gunshot," said Chase.

When Bodie had a chance to cross-examine the State's witness, he said, "There was a lot going on in the parking lot that night. A fight going on here; a fight over there. It must have been quite a violent, chaotic scene."

Even though Bodie had not framed his statement in the form of a question, Chase attempted to answer, saying, "Yes, sir. It was quite a mess."

Bodie resumed his stroll to the tall windows overlooking Third Street. He paused for a long, agonizing moment, either for emphasis, or to stare at the telephone wire drooping between poles. Two small birds were perched on the wire. They teetered and tilted and chirped. The red-capped male edged sideways, and as he drew near, the drab female, as if ticklish, skittered away. The persistent male came sidling along the wire once more, and this time he touched the tip of one wing to the female. When she did not shy away, he swung his head toward her and they touched beaks. Below the birds, on the ground, a number of trees were scattered around the courthouse lawn. At some point in the past, the trees had been badly pruned and welts and scars were evident where gray limbs had been improperly severed. On the street, passing to the west, was a lone pickup truck pulling a single-horse trailer. Bodie continued to stare out the window, his back to the room. He raised his voice and asked, "And what did you do to stop the fight, Mr. Chase?"

"Nothing. We cleared the hell out of there," said Chase.

Bodie swung his body until he faced the jury. He readjusted his glasses that had slipped a little, pushing them up on his nose. He started to move in the direction of the defense table while mumbling a single word, making sure he said it loud enough to be audible. The word was, "Coward."

Judge Foley gave Bodie a look of sudden alarm. He instructed the jury to disregard the last statement made by the defense counsel and admonished Bodie, saying, "You shall refrain from making such prejudicial comments in the future, Mr. Bodie." Judge Foley was furious and his words carried a sharp bite.

"Yes, sir," said Bodie politely as he took his seat.

*****

When Lee Rhoden, a local rancher, took the stand he claimed he had seen very little of the fight, and did not have a vivid memory of anything in particular. Bodie used his cross-examination as an opportunity to browbeat Rhoden, insinuating Rhoden had been gutless in refusing to come to the aid of Larry Irwin. Bodie snapped in mock revulsion, "I have no more questions of this witness."

As Bodie crossed the room to the defense table, he hooked his thumbs in the lapel of his suit coat and walked slowly while looking directly at Judge Foley. Bodie said nothing, but if not spoken, the word *coward* was once again definitely implied and hung like an ugly black cloud over the courtroom. Judge Foley leaned back in his chair. It was palpable he wanted to say something, but he refrained from saying anything.

*****

On the third day of the trial, the prosecution attempted to reenact the shooting—Shepard playing the part of Harvey, and Robinson playing the part of Griffith—but their efforts proved a dismal failure. Instead of the jury witnessing the severity of the shooting, the drama seemed more like a playground stunt and elicited laughter from the audience, as well as from the jury.

The prosecution, nearing the end of its presentation, recalled Lee Rhoden to the stand to further explain his testimony from the previous day. With a night to think it over, Rhoden's memory was much sharper. He related having witnessed Jimmy Bothum stagger backwards, and recalled seeing Griffith chasing Irwin toward the parking meters, sparring with him now and then as Irwin tried to get away.

During cross-examination Bodie removed his glasses and tossed them onto the table. He looked in the direction of the jury as he asked, "Was Griffith in any shape to inflict any damage to Irwin?"

"A man of Griffith's size is bound to do some damage," said Rhoden. He went on to say that he recalled Larry Irwin, "broke and ran, dodging around the parking meters. Ronnie Raymond came rushing toward him. Griffith was up and walking slowly away, wiping blood from his eyes. It was at that point Griffith fell to the ground."

Upon further questioning from Bodie, Rhoden testified it appeared to him as if Duane Harvey was fumbling with what might have been a pistol. Harvey then walked briskly toward the south end of the parking lot where Irwin and Raymond were fighting.

"Again," said Bodie, "you did nothing to stop the fight, or come to the aid of a man you had been introduced to, a man who had identified himself as an Oregon State Police officer?"

"Like I said yesterday, I didn't want to get involved any more than I already was," said Rhoden.

"Did you know Griffith had been shot, Mr. Rhoden?"

"From the way he went down, I suspected it," said Rhoden.

"And what was your reaction?" asked Bodie.

"I sure as hell didn't wanna get in the middle of a shooting match," said Rhoden.

As if appalled at Rhoden's lack of compassion, Bodie shook his head and decisively announced he had no further questions.

*****

After his experiences in the courtroom, Lee Rhoden felt as though Bodie had treated him unfairly. For the remainder of his life, he refused to have any dealings with Bodie, turning away when they met on the street or in a social setting.

*****

J.D. Brown was called to the stand. He said he had taken an upstairs room—number 228—in the Ochoco Inn on the night of December 15, 1964. His window overlooked the parking lot. He testified he was in bed reading, and at approximately

1:00 a.m. on the morning of December 16, 1964, he heard loud voices and looked outside to see what was going on. But the parking lot was dimly lit, and he saw nothing. He returned to bed and continued to read his book.

"About a minute or so later, I heard what sounded like a single gunshot," said Brown. "I put on my robe and shoes, and went to the landing to look out the window facing north. I saw a car parked in the alley, facing me. Two men were going toward the car. One man was wearing a white sweater, and he had his arm around the other man's shoulders. This fellow—he wore dark clothes—had his arm around the waist of the man with the white sweater. They both got in the front seat on the driver's side."

On cross-examination Bodie asked if the man in the white sweater appeared to need help in order to walk. Brown said yes, that the man in the white sweater appeared injured and unable to walk under his own power.

Several more witnesses were called. Patrolman Bill Hollowell testified he was the first officer to arrive on the scene after Griffith was shot. Jim Jones, Prineville city patrolman, was questioned briefly about his conversation in the Rustler's Roost with Larry Irwin, Ron Crawford and Jerry Hubbard.

Dr. Evan Jones, Crook County Medical Examiner, testified he pronounced Mac Griffith dead approximately 20 minutes after he was admitted to Pioneer Memorial Hospital. Shepard asked the doctor what he had done to try to save Griffith's life, and Dr. Evans replied, "I performed a tracheotomy to aid in breathing and was putting fluid into a leg vein to increase circulatory volume, when lack of heart action, as recorded by a cardiogram machine, indicated death had occurred."

"Will you tell us the injuries the victim sustained?" asked Shepard.

"Multiple bruises about the face and head, a cut on his hand and a skinned shoulder," said Dr. Jones. "The bullet entered the right anterior of the chest. The autopsy was performed by Dr. McGeary at my request."

*****

Dr. George McGeary, the Bend pathologist who performed the autopsy on Mac Griffith's body at the Prineville Funeral Home, testified the full cause of death was "hemorrhaging in the chest cavity, caused by the bullet's entry in the right anterior. The bullet did extensive damage to major blood vessels. Although there were extensive bruises on the scalp and face, no skull fracture or brain injury was discovered. I did observe a deep laceration on the ring finger of the right hand which exposed the tendon."

Bodie seized on this information and on cross-examination directed a question to Dr. McGeary, asking, "In your professional opinion, would such an injury to the right hand be caused by a vicious blow delivered by Mr. Griffith?"

"Mr. Griffith must have hit someone, or some thing, very hard in order to cause such a wound on the finger," said Dr. McGeary. He went on to say, "The backs of both of Mr. Griffith's hands were scratched and bruised."

"I think that indicates Mr. Griffith used his fists quite a lot that evening," said Bodie. "Dr. McGeary, how many autopsies have you performed and how many of those have involved gunshot wounds to the chest?"

"Approximately 2,000 autopsies, and probably a couple dozen of those involved gunshot wounds to the chest," said Dr. McGeary.

Upon return from the noon recess, Judge Foley made an announcement, saying he had just been informed it was in direct violation of the fire code to allow spectators to stand in the courtroom. He ordered anyone who was not seated to immediately leave. There was an audible groan from the audience, and those not seated shuffled their feet and departed the courtroom.

The prosecution and defense sparred as the attorneys quibbled back and forth on several points of law. Eventually they settled their differences when, in order to speed up the proceedings, the defense agreed to stipulate that the derringer pistol, offered as an exhibit by the prosecution, was found in a tree 28 miles west of Prineville; that the weapon was owned by the defendant, Duane Harvey; and the bullet removed from Griffith's body was from the defendant's gun.

The State called Lieutenant Manuel Boys, director of the Oregon State Crime Laboratory in Portland, who testified the blood sample taken from Mac Griffith's body had been tested, and the result was the blood sample contained .23 percent alcohol by weight.

On cross-examination Bodie asked, "With a blood alcohol of .23, would you consider Mr. Griffith to have been legally intoxicated?" The lieutenant, after answering in the affirmative, was allowed to step down.

A slide projector had been set up in the courtroom and the prosecution was prepared to project images onto a white, pull-down screen, pictures of Mac Griffith's body taken during the early morning hours of December 16, 1964. Bodie objected. Judge Foley directed the attorneys to meet him in his chambers. An hour and a half passed before they returned. Judge Foley ruled that five of the photographs could be shown to the jury. After warming up the projector, Shepard advanced the first slide. Although the light conditions were poor—the room was flooded with bright afternoon sunlight—the projected images were visible and very graphic. There was a photograph showing the head of the deceased, the bluish skin covered with ugly bruises the color of squashed plums; a close-up of the injured ring finger cut to white bone; the round bullet hole in the front of the chest; the back of the victim showing the surgical cut where the bullet was removed from under the skin; and the last photograph showed the path the bullet had taken through the lungs and into the rib. The room was absolutely silent except for the whirr of the projector's fan, and the distinct and chilling click as slides encased in cardboard dropped from the plastic carousel into the viewing chamber. Doug Shepard snapped the advance one more time. The screen returned to white. He turned off the light, but allowed the projector fan to continue running as the machine cooled. He addressed Judge

Foley, and in a loud, firm voice, he stated, "Your honor, the prosecution rests its case."

After a 15 minute recess, the defense sprang into motion with Bodie calling Sergeant L.H. Brockway, the supervisor of the Bend office of the Oregon State Police to the stand. He appeared very distinguished in his sergeant's uniform. Bodie asked him a single question. "Sergeant Brockway, in your professional opinion, what do you know about the reputations of Mac Griffith and Ronnie Raymond?"

"Bad," said the sergeant.

"Would you elaborate for us?" asked Bodie.

"Both the men you mentioned have well-known reputations among law enforcement as troublemakers," said Sergeant Brockway. "They are known to be barroom brawlers, and they are not easy to deal with from the side of law enforcement officers."

Bodie had no further questions, nor did Shepard or Robinson. Sergeant Brockway was allowed to step down. In quick succession Bodie called additional witnesses who testified about Griffith's and Raymond's reputations as fighters: Milford Mooney, Redmond Police Chief; Hugh Dragich, owner of Cecil's Pastime Bar; and David E. Joyle, Grant County Court Reporter. Shepard vehemently objected to the strategy employed by the defense, saying the defense was attempting to paint the victim as the villain. The defense and prosecution sparred for nearly an hour, with Judge Foley reprimanding both attorneys on numerous occasions. Rather than fight to counteract the defense, and insisting witnesses be called to testify to Griffith's good character, and his many redeeming qualities—the fact he was a married man and the father of a child, his general love of children, his respect for animals, his generosity and his status as a rodeo star—Shepard gave in to Bodie's bullying tactics. He submissively agreed to stipulate that Griffith and Raymond had *bad reputations* and were prone to *aggressive activities* when they were drinking alcohol. This stipulation was a turning point in the trial, akin to a wrestling match when one of the wrestlers cries *uncle* and gives up. By stipulating, the defense conceded that Mac Griffith was a bully and a troublemaker and his killing was most likely justified because he *had it coming*.

*****

In a booming voice, Bodie announced, "I have one more witness to call to the stand, the defendant, Duane Harvey."

This news electrified the crowd, and a gasp was audible. All eyes shifted toward the defense table as Duane Harvey slowly got to his feet, and walked the short distance to the front of the courtroom.

The man raising his right hand was slightly built and dressed fashionably in a white shirt, dark tie and a new blue suit. He had a fresh haircut, and his hair was neatly combed. He took his seat in the witness chair, looked to his left and smiled. It was not a contrived, tight-lipped smile intended to influence the members of the jury who would be deciding his fate, but a genuine and disarming smile. Bodie went right to work, asking the defendant a series of seemingly irrelevant questions: his date of birth, service record and when he had moved back to Prineville. Harvey testified he was born in 1931, had served in the United States Air Force for 10 years and six months, was honorably discharged and had returned to Prineville in 1963. Bodie asked where he was employed. Harvey said he was a mechanic helper, employed by Johnny Bushard at Central Auto Garage in Prineville. Bodie then inquired about Harvey's eyesight. Harvey responded without hesitation, "My vision is 20-20."

"What was your life like growing up?" asked Bodie.

"Good," said Harvey. No trace of a smile remained. "My parents divorced when I was 2 years old, and for 16 years I lived with Momma, Flora—he pointed to her sitting in the front row, her eyes swollen, dabbing at her tears with a handkerchief— and my stepfather, Homer Higgins. We lived in Prineville. I graduated from Crook County High School."

With these perfunctory and seemingly innocuous questions out of the way, Bodie got down to the meat and potatoes of the defense's case. He asked Harvey about the derringer that had been used to kill Mac Griffith. Harvey replied he received the gun as a gift while he was in the military, that he had placed it in the glove compartment in his car, had never had a reason to use it, and in fact, had never shot it before that night, and furthermore, was not sure if it was even loaded.

"Were you a customer at the Cinnabar Lounge the night of December 15, 1964?" asked Bodie. Harvey said he did not go out often, but yes, he had gone to the Cinnabar that evening. Then Bodie boldly plunged forward, asking if Harvey was aware, that as Mac Griffith and Larry Irwin were exiting the bar, they were going outside to engage in a fistfight.

"Yes, sir," said Harvey.

"And did you follow them?" asked Bodie.

"Not directly," said Harvey. "It seemed like trouble was brewing, and I felt it was a good time for me to leave. Anyway, it was getting late, and I had to be at work in the morning. When I stepped outside, I was surprised not to find Griffith and Irwin on Main Street. As I went to my car, I noticed two men, who I recognized as Ronnie Raymond and Jim Bothum, exit the Cinnabar, and walk hurriedly up Main Street, turning the corner onto Fourth Street."

"What did you do?" asked Bodie.

"I got into my car and started it. I was going to drive to my room at the Hacienda, but then decided on an impulse to circle the block. I turned east onto Fourth Street," said Harvey. "I continued to the entrance of the Ochoco Inn parking lot, and upon seeing a group of people standing in the parking lot—three or four men—I pulled into the driveway."

"Why did you pull into that parking lot driveway, Mr. Harvey?" asked Bodie.

"I was well aware of the reputations of Griffith, Raymond and Bothum as *fighting cowboys* who operated as a gang," said Harvey. "I was also aware that Griffith was a professional fighter. I was concerned the three cowboys might gang up on the state cop, Larry Irwin."

"And what did you see?" asked Bodie.

"I saw Griffith lying prone on the ground, face up, and Irwin was sitting on his chest," said Harvey. "He wasn't hitting Griffith. He was just sitting there on top of him. Raymond and Bothum were standing to the north. I did not get out of my car immediately. I was afraid to. At that point the odds were three-to-one, and I knew three-to-two wouldn't be a whole lot better. I'm not ashamed to admit it, but I'm not much of a fighter, and I was a little scared."

Harvey told his story, and at times it seemed as though Bodie urged that story along—the story limping forward in short, slow stages like an old man climbing a steep hill and in need of periodic encouragement—allowing the telling to unfold in practiced layers, just as it had been rehearsed many times. The defendant's testimony was absolutely crucial, and would more than likely be the deciding factor that could make or break the case. Harvey and Bodie played it perfectly. Harvey came across as straightforward, sincere and believable. Bodie appeared to be genuinely sympathetic.

Harvey said, "Jim Bothum made a lunging motion forward, and Irwin backed off. The second time Bothum tried the maneuver, Raymond grabbed him by his shoulders and physically restrained him. The third time Bothum lunged, Irwin, who had gotten up from where he was sitting on Griffith, swung on Bothum and knocked him down. I heard Raymond shout, 'You can't do that! I'll get you for that!'"

"What do you think Raymond meant by that statement?" prompted Bodie.

"It was apparent to me, Raymond was saying he was going to get Irwin for hitting Bothum," said Harvey.

"And what happened next?"

"Griffith jumped to his feet, and went into a fighter's stance. Irwin turned away and ran. Both Griffith and Raymond began chasing Irwin. Irwin made a dash toward the hotel, the back door. Raymond was chasing him, but Griffith gave up the chase and turned away, walking toward the center of the parking lot.

"Irwin kept running, and Raymond was near enough to slug him. Irwin stumbled, regained his balance, and kept running. It was apparent Irwin was winded, and I could clearly see Raymond was going to overtake him within a short distance. I hollered, 'Hey, Raymond! Stop it!'"

"Why did you shout at Raymond to stop it?" asked Bodie.

"I was hoping, if Raymond heard his name called, and knew someone was watching, he would stop and give up his chase," said Harvey.

"And what effect did it have?" asked Bodie.

"No effect, none at all," said Harvey. "Raymond leaped onto Irwin's back, driving him face-first onto the pavement. Raymond was astride of Irwin. He grabbed Irwin by the hair, and pounded his head up and down against the pavement. Irwin offered no resistance, but at one point I distinctly heard him call out, 'Help! Someone help! They're killing me!'"

"While Irwin was being severely beaten, what were Griffith and Bothum doing?" asked Bodie.

"Griffith and Bothum had come together and were advancing directly toward me," said Harvey. "One of them threatened me, saying, 'Oh, so you want some of this, too!' It was then I remembered the gun in the glove compartment of my car. I got the gun with the idea of bluffing the cowboys into stopping the fight. I pulled the gun out of the holster. I was holding the holster in my left hand and the gun in my right. Both arms were hanging down at my sides.

"Maybe Griffith saw the gun. He dropped into a crouching position with his fists doubled up, and his arms forward as if he was ready to fight."

"What did you do?" asked Bodie

"I shouted, 'Call Raymond off before he kills him,'" said Harvey. "The two men kept coming. Then Griffith growled, 'Okay, you son of a bitch, it's your turn.' Bothum backed him up, laughing and saying, 'That shouldn't be too hard, he's all alone.' I glanced toward Irwin and Raymond, and saw that Raymond was still swinging and Irwin was offering no resistance. When I looked back toward Griffith and Bothum, they were nearly upon me.

"I raised my arm to hip level—the derringer was still in my hand, pointing at an angle toward the ground—and shouted, 'Stop! That's far enough! Call Raymond off!'

"Griffith sneered and told me, 'You won't shoot; you're too damn scared. I'll take that gun and shove it down your throat, and then I'll stomp your guts out!'

"They advanced even closer. I hollered, 'Stop!' but they kept coming. I don't know how far away from me they were, maybe eight or ten steps. The next thing I knew I had raised the pistol—I don't know when I cocked and fired the gun—but Griffith did stop. He never said anything, just bent at the waist, staggered to one side, and started to go down. I really didn't know if he was hit, of if he was faking it. I watched him out of the corner of my eye; while I pointed my gun at Bothum's legs and ordered him to stop the fight, to get Raymond off Irwin.

"At that particular moment, I felt that my well-being, my life, was in imminent danger. I knew in my own mind, Irwin was also in danger of being killed. I was the only one who could save him."

Bodie allowed that charged statement to hang in the air for a long moment, and then he launched into a rambling discourse; reiterating once again that Mac Griffith and Ronnie Raymond were notorious brawlers. Then Bodie switched and began lauding praise on Harvey, commending him for his courage, and his honorable actions in protecting the life of Larry Irwin. Bodie concluded his remarks by reading very slowly and deliberately, clearly annunciating each word of the Oregon Revised Statutes, 161.209, "A person is justified in using physical force upon another person for self-defense, or to defend a third person from what the person reasonably believes to be the use, or imminent use, of unlawful physical force, and the person may use a degree of force which the person reasonably believes to be necessary for the purpose."

On cross-examination, Shepard tried to get Harvey to admit he had gone to the parking lot because he was mad that his ex-wife, Mary Edgerly, had been so attentive to Griffith. Harvey denied it. Shepard suggested Griffith's actions toward Pat Leonard, and her rebuke—telling Harvey not to tell her how to run a bar and she would not tell him how to mechanic—had also inflamed Harvey's passions. Again, Harvey denied the accusations.

"Mr. Harvey, you could have gotten back in your car and left the parking lot at any time, but you chose to stay," said Shepard. "Rather than leave what you had determined in your mind was a dangerous situation, you stayed. Can you tell this court why you stayed? Can you tell this court why you killed a man?"

"I'm sure they would have killed Larry Irwin," offered Harvey. "They might very well have killed me."

At this point in the trial, the prosecution continued to maintain that Harvey killed Griffith in a jealous rage. It did seem as though Harvey cared about both women, and that Griffith did pose a potential threat to Harvey's relationships with these women. But while making that the focus of the prosecution, other possibilities were not explored, and opportunities were allowed to slip away. What had been Harvey's decision-making process, especially in light of his alcoholic consumption? What direct threat had Griffith posed, when by Harvey's own admission Griffith was between 25 to 30 feet away from him? Why had Harvey felt compelled to arm himself when a prudent man would have simply driven to the police station, only a block away, to report the fight? Shepard returned to the table he shared with Fred Robinson. The two men spoke briefly, and then Shepard sat down and told Judge Foley, "No further questions, Your Honor."

*****

The defense immediately rested its case and Judge Foley called for closing arguments. The prosecution went first. Shepard outlined the State's case against Harvey. He methodically went through the evidence, item by item, and pointed out Harvey's admission he had shot Griffith. And once again he contended Harvey had pulled the trigger out of jealousy, protectiveness and passion. He held members of the jury in rapt attention as he brandished the deadly derringer pistol that had fired the fatal bullet. He paced back and forth with that weapon for several minutes, demonstrating over and over again how the weapon had to be removed from the holster, cocked and then fired. Three times, while theatrically pulling the trigger each time, he repeated Harvey's own words, "I don't know when I cocked and fired the gun."

Shepard did attempt to discount Larry Irwin's testimony that he had called for help while being beaten by Ronnie Raymond. "When you are getting a severe beating, and drifting in and out of consciousness," Shepard contended, "you don't yell for help." He pointed in the direction of Larry Irwin, seated in the audience, and said with his voice rising sharply, "Look at that man. He was trained by the Army as an elite member of a top secret military unit. You saw the way he moves. He moves across a room like a panther. There is no one in this courtroom better able to defend himself than is Larry Irwin. He did not need Duane Harvey's help. Larry Irwin was perfectly capable of defending himself. What it comes down to is this— no individual in this society has the right to take the law into his own hands. What happened in this case is that Mr. Harvey took it upon himself to be the judge, jury and executioner. Plain and simple, he alone made the decision to pull that trigger. He alone is responsible for the murder of Mac Griffith."

Shepard walked to his chair and wearily took his seat. He waited for the cagy veteran, Jim Bodie, to launch his summation. Shepard remained confident in the fact that the prosecution would be allowed a final rebuttal before the jury deliberated.

As Bodie began his dramatic closing, his Southern accent thickened and he sometimes gestured wildly with his hands. He ranted about injustice, saying his client should never have been arrested. He pleaded and beseeched the jury to see Harvey not as a murderer, but as a genuine American hero. He stated, "Mr. Harvey feared for his life and exhibited immense courage in coming to the aid of his fellow man, a state policeman who was being brutally assaulted."

Bodie became even more animated and emotional in his delivery. Tears welled at the corners of his eyes, and tears spilled down his ruddy cheeks. He did not attempt to wipe them away, but he wore those tears as though they were badges of honor. He pressed forward, saying this particular case had disturbed and distressed him more than any case he had been involved in during his long and storied career as an attorney.

"If you and I don't have the moral fiber to help the helpless then we are worse than a pack of wild animals in the jungle," cried Bodie. "I pray to God, if this ever happens to me, to my child, or to any other human being, that I have the guts to do whatever I can to protect the innocent among us. I pray to God I have the guts to stand my ground as Mr. Harvey stood his ground."

The *Bend Bulletin* newspaper reported, "Defense attorney, James Bodie, impatient and somewhat crusty throughout the trial, drew surprise murmurs from the crowded courtroom as he twice dissolved in tears as he was giving his summation. He broke down completely at its conclusion and hurried from the courtroom."

After Bodie stormed from the room, Jim Minturn got to his feet, and it quickly became evident his courtroom demeanor contrasted markedly from that of Bodie. Minturn, who had grown up in Oregon, was easily understood by the jury. The words he chose to use were down-to-earth and folksy. He was quietly persuasive, almost methodical in his delivery as he systematically reviewed the case. When finished with the facts he said, "The prosecution contends Mr. Irwin had nothing to say as he lay on the ground being beaten to death. I want to tell you, if I'm in a fight, and I'm the one on the ground, I holler. I holler at the top of my lungs. I holler so loud the whole world can hear me." Some members of the jury, especially the men, smiled at this admission.

Minturn persisted, "During the week this trial has lasted, I've sat here and listened to both sides debate the case. I have heard details presented in this courtroom that I was not previously aware of. Until a couple months ago, I was the Crook County District Attorney. I know what Mr. Shepard has gone through in preparing and presenting his side. I admire him for his skills in attempting to make a case for the State.

"I have heard all the evidence, just as you have. I feel as though I am like the 13th juror. And as an impartial 13th juror I see gaping holes in Mr. Shepard's case. If I had been in his shoes, I do not believe I would ever have advanced this case to trial. It is a case the State cannot hope to win.

"Let us begin by taking an unbiased look at the Cinnabar Lounge in the early morning hours of December 16, 1964. The atmosphere was ripe for trouble. If the defendant, Mr. Harvey, had been looking for trouble, he had ample opportunity to find it in the bar that night. The rough-hewn men in the bar—those *cowboys*—make their living in a world of violence. They crawl on the backs of wildly bucking broncs and bulls. In addition, each of these three men have built individual reputations for fighting and hurting people. They can say what they want, but Ronnie Raymond and Jim Bothum were not going out for a cup of coffee when they left the bar that night. They were on their way to find the fight that was going on between Griffith and Irwin. They planned to join in that fight, to gang up on Larry Irwin, if that proved necessary.

"We can reason now, seven weeks after the fact, what should have been done, but the defendant did not have the luxury of time. He was in a dire situation where he feared for his life, as well as the life of another. He had to make an instantaneous decision—he *had to*—a decision that would ultimately save his life, and the life of his fellow man.

"Ladies and gentlemen of the jury, allow me the indulgence of bringing to you a case that recently happened in New York City that you may, or may not, be aware of." Minturn picked up a copy of *Time* magazine lying face down on the defense table. He held it up and paraded in front of the jury box making sure each individual looked at the cover where a young woman, a brunette with close-cropped hair and an innocent smile, was pictured. He returned the magazine to the table.

"Catherine Susan 'Kitty' Genovese was born July 3, 1935," said Minturn. "She was the eldest of five children of a family living in a lower-middle class Italian American section of Brooklyn. Kitty graduated from high school, and at the time of her death, was working at Ev's Eleventh Hour Sports Bar on Jamaica Avenue and 193rd Street in Queens, New York. She lived in an apartment near her place of employment.

"In the early morning hours of March 13, 1964, after closing down the bar, Kitty arrived at the parking lot of her apartment. As she approached the door, a man jumped out of the shadows. Kitty ran, but the man caught her and stabbed her in the back with a knife. Kitty screamed at the top of her lungs, 'Oh my God, he stabbed me! Help me!' Over and over again she screamed, and cried for help. Neighbors got up from their beds and peered outside.

"It was reported that 38 onlookers witnessed the brutal attack. Only one man even bothered to intercede, and he merely shouted at the attacker, 'Let that girl alone!' Nobody else bothered to come to the aid of this young woman as she was repeatedly stabbed, and then as she lay dying, her attacker savagely raped her. Not one of those 38 men and women, as reported in *Time* magazine, attempted to come to the aid of Kitty Genovese. She suffered knife wounds to her hands and arms as she valiantly attempted to fight off her attacker. But her struggles proved futile. She died in the ambulance while en route to the hospital.

"We might ask ourselves, how has our society become so callous that it would permit such a heinous crime to be committed while onlookers stand idly by, doing nothing? Is it fear, insensitivity, apathy? One neighbor coldly stated, 'I didn't want to get involved.' We heard that same statement in this courtroom. I didn't want to get involved. Another witness turned up his radio so he did not have to hear the screams of the young woman as she valiantly fought for her life. Thirty-eight onlookers and not one of those individuals had the guts to step forward.

"I am beginning to wonder if those bystanders in New York City were not the smart people. They turned their backs. They refused to become involved. And here we are in Prineville, Oregon, holding a trial for a man who could have walked away, and not become involved. If Mr. Harvey had simply walked away from that deadly confrontation in the parking lot behind the Ochoco Inn, he would not be in this courtroom today fighting for justice, fighting to preserve his good name and upstanding reputation, fighting for his own life.

"There were no charges filed against Mac Griffith for his violent behavior, or the violent behavior of his *cowboy* buddies that night. Yet we are here, trying this man for murder when all he is guilty of is acting within his rights according to the Constitution of the United States of America, and the laws of the State of Oregon. He had every right to protect himself, and if he deemed it necessary, to become involved and save the life of his fellow man.

"Where are we as a society when we seek to punish those with the moral fiber exhibited by this defendant, the man who made a stand for justice? I ask you, if you were put in the same position as Duane Harvey, what would you have done? You feel your life is being threatened, and you hear a man calling for help. 'Help! Help! They're killing me! They're killing me!' You make a split-second decision—will you be a coward and run away, or do you stand your ground?—Duane Harvey stood his ground.

"Ladies and gentlemen of the jury, maybe murder while onlookers stand idly by is acceptable behavior in New York City, but by God, in Crook County, Oregon, it is not acceptable behavior. Here, we come to the aid of our fellow man. I urge you—I implore you—to bring back a verdict of not guilty by reason of self-defense."

*****

Shepard followed with his rebuttal, but in reality, everything had already been said and the die had been cast. Judge Foley instructed the jury, advising them on the points of law they were to consider in making their decision. He wished the jurors well on reaching a verdict, and praised them, saying he hoped they revered the institution of the jury system as much as he did. Then he excused them to begin deliberations.

*****

It took the jury less than two hours to return a verdict. Dick Hoppes, jury foreman, read the verdict in a loud, clear voice, saying, "We, the members of the jury do hereby find the defendant, Duane Harvey," he paused momentarily, and then announced, "not guilty of the charge of second degree murder."

The *Bend Bulletin* reported, "Upon the reading of the verdict, Mrs. Flora Wilcox, Duane Harvey's mother and a front row spectator throughout the trial, cried, 'Thank God!' She collapsed into the arms of relatives, and sat with her eyes closed and her hands held in an attitude of prayer."

The *Bend Bulletin* also reported, "Larry Irwin, former State Police recruit, whose life Harvey said he was attempting to save when he shot rodeo star Mac Griffith, hurried to the defendant's side with tears in his eyes."

Dick Hoppes, circa 1970

The Jury Foreman

Dick Hoppes had been a cowboy, but once he and Barbara were married and had started a family, he gave up participating in the sport of rodeo and concentrated on his laundry business in Prineville. Dick owned and operated Hoppes Laundry and Cleaners. On the morning of December 16, 1964, Dick was working in the laundry boiler room, stoking the fire, when the mortician from the Prineville Funeral Home walked in and asked Dick a very strange and macabre question; whether he would like to view the most perfect physical specimen of a man he would ever see.

"I've always been squeamish about blood and dead bodies, but for some odd reason I walked across the alley to the funeral home," said Dick. "The mortician had already performed the blood-letting, and whatever else needed to be done to prepare the body for shipment. The nude body was on a gurney, and I will say the man was well-muscled with broad shoulders and a narrow waist. His face had been badly beaten, and the backs

181

of his hands were swollen, scarred, skinned, scraped and cut. Those hands were huge. They looked like big, heavy weights attached to the ends of his arms. The mortician told me the body was legendary rodeo cowboy, Mac Griffith, a name I knew well. This may seem an odd thing for me to say, but even in death, Mac Griffith and those enormous hands of his, that perfectly sculpted body, seemed to give off a sense of lethal power.

"Seven weeks later, I was surprised when I was called to be in the jury pool for the trial of Duane Harvey, the man accused of killing Mac Griffith. I said in court that I had participated as a rodeo contestant, and thought I'd be promptly excused. Instead Jim Bodie asked if my experiences as a cowboy would influence my thinking, or sway my opinion one way or another. I said I believed I could be impartial, and judge the matter of innocence or guilt strictly on the facts as they were presented. I was surprised once again to be seated on the jury, and later I was absolutely shocked to be selected as the foreman.

"As the trial progressed, it became quickly apparent to those of us on the jury, that Jim Bodie was an excellent attorney. The thrust of his vigorous defense focused on the victim, portraying Mac Griffith as a tough cowboy who rode broncs and bulls and fought with his fists. Testimony established him as a formidable fighter, with some professional boxing experience. Bodie made a point of contrasting Mac Griffith against his client, Duane Harvey, a much smaller man, a veteran of the Air Force, a peacemaker who, when pitted against the cowboys, feared for his life and sought to protect the life of his fellow man, Larry Irwin. Harvey had reacted, according to Bodie, strictly in self-defense.

"What we learned in the courtroom was that on the night Griffith was killed, he was drinking heavily. Two off-duty state patrolmen were in the Cinnabar. One of the cops, Crawford, had enough sense to leave, but the other, Larry Irwin, stuck around and got in an altercation with Griffith. They went to the parking lot to fight.

"I remember Bodie asking Larry Irwin, since he was not an imposing man and had a rather slight build, how he could have knocked out a man the size of Mac Griffith. Irwin shrugged his shoulders, smiled confidently, said something to the effect that he had a good right, and Griffith must have had a glass jaw. People in the audience laughed at that remark, as they did again when the prosecution reenacted the shooting; one attorney said, 'Bang!' and the other attorney fell to the floor.

"Bodie made sure Duane Harvey was depicted as an innocent bystander. When Harvey was on the stand, he testified Griffith wanted to challenge everyone around, even after he was beaten by Irwin he still wanted to fight. Harvey became scared, and for self-protection, he went and got his gun from his car. Griffith came forward. Harvey reacted and fired his weapon. After the shooting, Harvey and Irwin drove to Bend. When Harvey told Irwin he might have shot a man, and that it was a .22 derringer, Irwin supposedly laughed and said not to worry, that a .22 slug might sting a man as big as Griffith, but it sure as hell wouldn't kill him. Another witness, a doctor, testified the bullet that killed Griffith had zigzagged around in his chest and tore up everything inside, including cutting an artery. He bled to death internally.

"My personal opinion of the trial was that Jim Bodie was an extremely competent attorney, and his arguments were convincing and persuasive. His questioning was direct and informative. He extracted from each witness the information that spotlighted his client, and the actions of his client, in the most favorable light possible and skillfully avoided any testimony that might conflict with that. Mac Griffith was represented to be an extremely dangerous man who posed a serious threat of bodily harm to anyone who stood in his way. If a juror accepted the information solicited by Bodie at face value, then there was no other choice that could have been reached, except to have the verdict go in favor of the defense.

"Not to be critical of Doug Shepard, but he was inexperienced, had never before been involved in a murder trial, and it was difficult for him to counteract Bodie and his courtroom theatrics. If either of the men sitting at the prosecution table had been more seasoned, there is not a doubt in my mind the jury would have convicted Duane Harvey of second degree murder.

"Once the jury was sequestered, and I had been selected the jury foreman, I allowed everyone to have his or her say. There was a lengthy conversation among some of the jurors concerning the fact Harvey could have walked away, but chose to stay, and in addition had purposefully returned to his automobile and secured a gun. These actions caused some jurors to question if Harvey was actually acting in self-defense, or if he indeed was the aggressor. The second item of contention was that Harvey had hid the weapon; indicating he knew he had done something wrong. The jury debated the pros and cons of both points, and everyone had the opportunity to have his or her say.

"Taking the proverbial bull by the horns, I told the predominantly female jury that it would be difficult to judge how any person might react under stress; and that Harvey reacting a certain way in hiding the weapon, did not indicate guilt or innocence. I posed a question to the members of the jury, asking if they were faced with a similar situation, would they get rid of the gun? And while they were mulling this over, I tackled the thorny issue of whether or not Harvey had acted in self-defense when he shot Mac Griffith. I said, according to Oregon law, ORS statute 161.209, a person has a right to defend themselves, or a third party, if they feel their life, or the life of another, is in jeopardy. I read the law aloud, and stated that Harvey's actions were consistent with a strict adherence to the definition of self-defense. It would appear, according to Harvey's testimony about his frame of mind at the time of the shooting, that he was defending himself, and defending the life of his fellow man.

"I called for a vote. We needed 10 of the 12 jurors to agree on a verdict, and if memory serves me, the vote was unanimous. I read the verdict and Harvey's family rushed to congratulate him. It was pandemonium.

"It took me a few minutes to search out Doug Shepard. I felt compelled to say a few things to him, and told him point blank, 'Young man, a word of advice is in order. As a jury, our only choice was guilt or innocence on a single count of murder two, but if you would have given us the option of intentional manslaughter, unintentional manslaughter, or involuntary manslaughter, we would have found the defendant guilty of a lesser charge.'

"I walked down the courthouse steps and members of the Griffith family were gathered on the sidewalk. They never said anything directly to me, but I could tell by the way they glared at me they were upset at the outcome, just as I would have been. I imagine some people around town thought Harvey got away with murder, but that didn't seem to be a bothersome thing—life went on like always, and Harvey walked away a free man in the eyes of the law."

Jim Straughn, 2014

The Kid

Charlie Straughn, and his wife, Mary Lou, owned and operated the Hacienda Motel, a pumice block and stucco set of buildings with distinctive red roofs located on the west end of Prineville near the bridge over the Crooked River. Duane Harvey rented a room with a kitchenette at the eight-unit motel. He was a good tenant, polite and mild-mannered. He always paid his rent on time.

"I woke up the morning of December 16, 1964, listening to the local radio station, KRCO, like I always did," said Jim Straughn, who at that time was a 17-year-old senior at Crook County High School. "On *Hometown News,* it was announced a shooting had occurred at the Cinnabar Lounge, and Duane Harvey had been arrested at the Hacienda Motel, and was being charged with murder one. I ran to tell Dad. Wanting to know if it was true, we knocked on Duane's door—no answer—so Dad used his pass key to open the door. We looked inside and blood was everywhere: bloody handprints on the walls, spots of blood dripped on the floor, blood on the bedspread, bloody towels, and the sink looked like it belonged in a butcher shop. Dad remarked, 'What the hell happened here?' We didn't know. We thought someone had been murdered in the room.

"Dad made me go to school that day. My friends had learned some of the details of the shooting and they told me Duane and a cop had been drinking at the Cinnabar when a group of cowboys came in and started causing trouble. The *cowboy mentality* was prevalent around Prineville, and if you were in the company of cowboys, you better be rough and ready. I heard stories of cowboys sweeping through a barroom and knocking hats off people, stealing drinks, things like that; just generally harassing people, looking for a fight and acting like bullies on a playground.

"According to the rumors that circulated, Mac Griffith, a well-known rodeo superstar, got into a fistfight with a cop, and the cop damn near beat him to death. The only person to stand up to the cowboys was Duane. He pulled a pistol from the glove compartment of his car—he was driving a red Ford Falcon—and challenged Mac Griffith. Duane's only choice was to pull the trigger. After the shooting, Duane brought the cop to his room and tried to clean him up before driving him to the hospital in Bend. That was where the blood had come from—the cop. Duane returned to his room, and was arrested that morning. We slept through the whole thing, missed it all.

"Duane was the talk of the town, and the general consensus of opinion seemed to be one of understanding. Most folks viewed the cowboys—especially if they were drinking—akin to a pack of wild dogs; and the opinion was, although it was sad one of them had to die, he more than likely had it coming. I think that same mind-set must have prevailed with the jury too. Duane was found not guilty.

"After the verdict, Dad and Mom held a victory barbeque for Duane in the motel parking lot. Dad drank whiskey and cooked steaks. Mom and the others drank Oly beer. It was a small party, just our other two monthly tenants—Tom Nehls and Jerry Noble—and a handful of Duane's family and friends.

Duane stayed off by himself. He didn't seem to be in much of a celebrating mood; acted more like a shell-shocked soldier who had come back from the war. People congratulated him, but he didn't have much to say. I think he was just relieved to have it over and done with, and not be confined to jail.

"Two nights later, there was a hell of a big commotion in our motel parking lot. Two cars pulled in, cowboys poured out and they tried to kick in the door of Duane's room. Duane was there, but he was hiding. Dad yelled at Mom to call the cops, and then he stepped outside armed with his 12-gauge shotgun. He walked up to the cowboys and ordered them, 'Load up and get the hell off my property.' But they paid him no mind, kept kicking at the door, calling Duane names and challenging him to come out.

"Ronnie Raymond, a local legend, famous as a bronc rider and well-known as a general bad ass who liked to pick fights, was more or less the ringleader of the cowboys. Dad confronted Ronnie, shoved the end of the shotgun barrel into his ribs and told him to call off the cowboys. Ronnie did what he was told. What choice did he have? The cowboys loaded up and headed back into town.

"Dad admitted, after it was over, he had been scared to death. He said he was shaking so badly he hoped he wouldn't pull the trigger by accident. About a year later—I had finished school and was working at Boeing and living in Seattle– Ronnie caught up with Dad at the Pastime, pulled him off his bar stool and put the boots to him.

"Two years later—I had come to town and was having a drink at the Casino with my brother-in-law, Lyle Smith—in walked Ronnie Raymond. I started to get up, not that I'm tough or anything, but Ronnie needed to know the Straughn family didn't cotton to him beating up an old man. Lyle, who really was tough, shoved me down in my chair, growled, 'He's mine.' He got up and hit Ronnie so hard he knocked him off his feet and then Lyle stomped him like a bug.

"Craig and Brick Woodward were running the Casino for their dad, Ben, and Craig came over and asked if I wanted him to break up the fight. I told him, 'Not just yet,' and he let it go a little longer, just to even the score for Ronnie having beaten up Dad."

Duane Harvey, 2013

The Shooter

In 1964, Duane Claire Harvey was 33 years old, had served a 10-year stint in the Air Force, was honorably discharged and had returned to his hometown of Prineville. He had three failed marriages behind him, and except for a few traffic tickets—he owned fast cars and liked to drive them fast—he had never been in trouble with the law.

Mary Edgerly had been Duane's second wife. Duane said, "We were married when I was overseas; stationed in Japan and then Korea during the Korean War. I came home on leave and was told the bartender at the Casino Bar had been sleeping with my wife. I walked into the Casino and everyone was expecting an explosion. I'm sure the bartender thought I was there to kill him. But I pulled him off to one side and told him real quiet like, 'You may think I hate your guts; I've got every reason in the world to hate your guts, but to be honest with you, I'm here tonight to have a good time and I'm happy as hell you took that bad bitch off my hands.' There was no waiting period for divorce in Oregon; I divorced Mary while I was on leave."

After moving home to Prineville, Duane found employment working as a mechanic helper for Johnny Bushard in his automotive shop, Central Auto Garage, located at 129 West 4th Street, next door to Hoppes Laundry and Cleaners. Duane had very little mechanical experience, but could tear down a motor and pull a transmission. Before opening his own business, Johnny had worked a number of years for Ochoco Automotive. He was considered a good all-around mechanic. His specialty was automatic transmissions. As a businessman, Johnny had two glaring flaws; he liked to nip from a bottle while he worked, and he extended credit to customers who could not, or would not, pay their bills. As a result, Johnny became mired in financial difficulties and when he was unable to pay Duane the wages he had coming, he made it right by giving Duane a 1959 Cadillac. Duane drove the showboat with the tall tail fins for a few months, and traded it in for a red Ford Falcon. The Falcon was not the car Duane wanted, but it was what he could afford to own and operate.

Duane lived at the Hacienda Motel, on the west end of town. One month, when money was tight, Duane paid his rent in dimes. Duane said, "When I was in the Air Force and stationed in California, I worked during my off-duty hours driving taxi. The fellow who owned the company was crippled. His wife was a real looker, and we got to spending time together. One thing led to another, and we started sleeping together. I'm sure her husband knew about the situation, but he never said anything to me. In fact, he arranged for me to drive his wife all over Southern California. She was a coin collector and she liked to go to coin shows. She was the one who got me started collecting Mercury dimes. I had a big bag of them. The joke was—we called them *Harvey dimes*. One month I couldn't pay my rent at the Hacienda and I gave the Straughns my bag of *Harvey dimes*. I told them they would be valuable if they hung onto them for a few years. I don't know if they did or if they traded them in."

192

Duane was dating several women in Prineville, but because of his financial situation, he did not date often, nor did he frequent the bars in town. Johnny Bushard, who paid Duane only sporadically, gave Duane a draw the evening of December 15, 1964, and after having a couple of nips with Johnny at the automotive shop, Duane decided to swing by the Cinnabar Lounge and have a few more.

"I went to the Cinnabar and Pat Leonard was working," said Duane. "She and I were good friends and dated off and on. I was drinking vodka and Seven-Up, not drinking heavy, just steady. Mac Griffith was at the bar, pretty well tanked up; loud, belligerent and wanting to pick a fight. I didn't know him, didn't want to know him, and certainly didn't appreciate the way he talked to Pat. I told her to call the cops and kick his ass the hell out of the bar, but Pat said she could handle drunks.

"Two state cops, and another fellow from Bend, came into the bar and had a bite to eat in the Rustler's Roost, a room adjoining the bar. John Hudspeth and a few regular customers drifted in. Then two cowboys, Ronnie Raymond and his buddy, Jimmy Bothum, arrived and sat at the bar with Griffith. Ronnie was a few years older than me. He was trouble from the get-go. I stayed clear of Ronnie. Always figuring he could mind his own business, and I'd mind mine.

"The evening was going along just fine until John Hudspeth got in an argument and pulled a knife. Not wanting to see anyone get stuck, I picked up a chair to separate John and this other fellow. Someone got a cut, I don't remember who, but Hudspeth calmed down and bought the house a round of drinks. Everything got back to normal.

"Then Mac Griffith and Larry Irwin squared off and stepped outside to settle their differences. I got a feeling it was a good time for me to clear out. I got in my car with the intention of going home to my room at the Hacienda, but changed my mind on a whim, and decided to circle the block. I suppose I wanted to see about the fight. I certainly didn't want the cowboys ganging up on a state cop. I guess I went to check on his well-being.

"When I pulled into the parking lot behind the Ochoco Inn, I saw Larry Irwin had Mac Griffith on the ground and was punching him out. I noticed my ex-wife, Mary Edgerly, sitting in a car with Lee Rhoden and another fellow. I've been told she was in the bar that night dancing with Mac, but I don't remember her being there. The first time I remember seeing her was sitting in the car between the two guys. They were watching the fight. They had a ringside seat.

"The fight stopped. Irwin got up, and then Ronnie Raymond and Jimmy Bothum showed up and Raymond and Irwin got into a scuffle. Irwin tried to get away, ran to the far side of the parking lot, fighting with Raymond as he went. Raymond caught Irwin, knocked him to the ground and was hitting him.

"I've always been more of a lover than a fighter. I got back in my car, and I was going to drive to where the fight was going on between Raymond and Irwin. I was hoping I could stop it. But Griffith and Bothum were coming toward me in a very threatening way. One of them said something. I don't remember what was said, but I know what was in my mind; all those stories I'd heard about cowboys, how once they got you on the ground they put the boots to you, and you were likely to get cut, have bad bruises, broken bones, and maybe even brain damage, or get killed. Those cowboys had all been in trouble with the law on numerous occasions, and should have been strung up for some of the shit they pulled. I knew I was in a real dodgy situation. Hell, my life was at risk.

"Many years before, when I was in the service, someone gave me a little two-shot, .22 caliber derringer. I kept it in the glove compartment of my Falcon—had never fired it before that night—and wouldn't have bet money it was even loaded. I pulled the gun free from the leather holster. What I had on my mind, I think, was just to scare the cowboys, make them stop fighting the cop. I walked to the front of my car holding the pistol at my side, pointed down. Griffith must have seen it. He swore at me. Griffith and Bothum kept coming. I cocked the derringer, raised it to my hip and pulled the trigger without aiming, or even being aware of what I was doing. The gun went off. Griffith stopped coming, slumped over. Bothum took another step or two, and then he stopped, too. I ran to the back of the parking lot, to where Raymond had Irwin on the ground, and shouted for Raymond to stop. He jumped up and ran away. I got Irwin to his feet and helped him to my car. He was messed up, bleeding from cuts on his head and inside his mouth and missing some teeth.

"I got Irwin to my room at the Hacienda Motel, cleaned him up the best I could, and was going to take him to the Prineville hospital, but had second thoughts—the cowboys would probably have waylaid us—and drove to the hospital in Bend instead. That's what I remember about that night, but there are a lot of black spots in my memory. There are just things your memory wants you to forget.

"I do remember stopping somewhere between Prineville and Bend, and stashing the derringer in a juniper tree off the road. I don't know why I did that. I wasn't even sure whether or not I had hit Griffith. I sure as hell didn't know he was dead. I just wanted to get rid of the damn thing. I took Irwin to the hospital, waited for him, ran him to his apartment, and came home to the Hacienda and went to bed.

"The cops came for me early in the morning. They knocked on the door and told me I was under arrest for murder one. That was the first I knew Griffith was dead. I got dressed and went with them. They put me in jail. I stayed there until my stepfather, Homer Higgins, put up some property for collateral and Bodie sprung me.

"I think a lot of people in Prineville were on my side. I had more than one person say to me, 'Too bad you didn't kill 'em all.' Folks knew how bad the cowboys could be when they ganged up on an innocent person. That was common knowledge.

"My trial is one big blur to me. I know I was lucky to have had Jim Bodie and Jim Minturn on my side. Pat Taylor, my first ex-wife, arranged all that. Bodie was one of the best attorneys around. During the testimony he stuck to facts, was very businesslike; orderly, logical, precise and persuasive. He and Minturn did a good job, no question about that.

"After it was over, and I was found not guilty, I felt like someone had lifted a heavy weight off me. I could finally breathe again. It was a wonderful feeling, an uplifting experience. My family and friends were happy. They rushed to congratulate me, but what I remember most is looking over and seeing the way the Griffith people were glaring at me. I knew right then and there, I needed to watch my back or else someone was going to slip up and put a slug between my shoulder blades. It was pretty obvious, no matter what the jury had said, that there were people who still blamed me. Hell, they hated my guts.

"I really don't mind getting shot by some jealous husband—I'd figure I had it comin'—but I sure as hell don't want to get killed by a bunch of goddamn rodeo cowboys, especially after I was found innocent.

"After the verdict came down, the Straughns threw a party for me in the parking lot at the Hacienda Motel. Jesus, it was February and it was cold. They called it a *victory celebration,* but I didn't feel much like celebrating. A man was dead. He wasn't coming back to life. I was the one who pulled the trigger. And now, for the rest of my days, I'd have to live with that. If a fellow was to dwell on such a thing, it might drive him crazy.

"Some spooky shit happened to me in the weeks after the trial. One time a carload of cowboys chased me clear to Redmond. I stopped at a bar, parked, went in the front and right out the back door.

"Another time, Jimmy Bothum actually tried to jump me. My sister was down from Portland for a visit, and we went to the Cinnabar to have a drink. I saw Bothum come in and I told my sister whatever happened she was to sit tight and not get involved. Bothum saw me, mouthed off, started in my direction, and about halfway across the room he put his head down and charged me like a goddamn bull; straight at me with murder on his mind. I stepped to one side, grabbed hold of him by the back of his shirt and belt, and threw him head-first into the wall of glass bricks separating the bar from the Rustler's

Roost. That took a lot of the fight out of him. He got up all woozy, staggering around. I think he got the message that I wasn't quite the pushover he took me to be.

"I was told Bothum is still alive, living near Prineville, and he's a hard drinker. I doubt if I'd even recognize the son of a bitch if I saw him. I've tried to forget the bad. Bothum is one of those bads. If I ran into him, and knew who the hell he was, I'd buy that son of a bitch a fifth of whiskey and try to end his misery a little sooner rather than later.

"Supposedly Larry Irwin, on his death bed, claimed Bodie got him to lie on the stand. That's a crock of shit. If I was a member of the jury and heard he recanted his testimony, that wouldn't make me change my mind one iota, not if you knew what those *cowboys* were capable of. When I'm on my deathbed, I might say I was the one who dropped the bomb on Hiroshima, and I sure as hell wasn't. Irwin was just shooting off his mouth. Anyway, his testimony wasn't all that crucial. He sure as shit wasn't the one who got me off. Truth got me off.

"I just wish the whole goddamn mess had never happened. There is so much that night I can't remember—hell, don't want to remember—I suppose. Thinking about it brings up unpleasant feelings. I don't know why it happened, but it did. I took a man's life. Not that it makes any goddamn difference. What choice did I have? I acted to protect my life and the life of a state cop. That's all that needs to be said. Just that and the fact the jury said I was justified.

"Ask yourself this question, why is a good Samaritan a good Samaritan? Why doesn't a good Samaritan just mind his own goddamn business? Is it something inside him? I don't know, but in the shooting of Mac Griffith, I see myself as a good Samaritan. Not that I wanted to be or claimed to be. I just was.

"It still bothers me, the shooting does. I have nightmares. I'm there in the parking lot. My car is running. I'm standing in the headlights. Bothum and Griffith are coming at me. I raise my gun. I relive the whole goddamn memory of the thing. I do. And it always ends with a man lying dead on the ground.

It bothers the hell out of me. I wake up sweating and sick to my stomach.

"There are things we each have to live with—regrets. I regret I was ever at the Cinnabar that night. I regret having had to pull the trigger. Was it something that was supposed to happen? Was Mac Griffith scheduled to die that night? Was it fate? I think about it now and it seems like I was powerless to stop the sequence of events from happening. All I know is that I'm not a killer. I'm not a killer."

The End

Special Thanks

Marilyn Morrell, Albert Van Dorn, Betty Barnstetter, Bill Brewer, Bill Nichols, Dick Hoppes, Don Griffith, Doug Shepard, Duane Harvey, Durk Irwin, Monte Irwin, Gene Marr, Gibb Gregg, Harry Noble, Jim Bothum, Jerry Noble, Jim Minturn, Jim Straughn, Kelly McCommach, Larry Mahan, Marty Wood, Max Nogle, Mike Wallis, Monte Gibson, Pat Leonard, Rene Ledbetter, Rich Raymond, Ronnie Raymond, Sammy Flynn, Selma Adams, Sharon Lewis, Laura McShane, Steve Lent, Colleen Pedersen, Dick Pedersen, Donette Bailey, Debbie Peterson, Rick Lucas, Terry Romero, Jody Conners, Tom MacDonald, Kristine Taylor, Tim and Judy Grell, Bob and Wanda Frisby, John and Jeannie Martin, and Lynn Troupe.

Rick Steber, the author of more than thirty books and sales of more than a million copies, has received national acclaim for his writing. His numerous awards include the Western Writers of America Spur Award for Best Western Novel, Independent Publishers Award—Best Regional Fiction, Western Heritage Award, Benjamin Franklin Award, Mid-America Publishers Award, Oregon Library Association Award and Oregon Literary Arts Award. Two of his books have been optioned to movie production companies.

In addition to his writing, Rick is an engaging Western personality and has the unique ability to make his characters come alive as he tells a story. He has spoken at national and international conferences and visits schools where he talks to students about the importance of education, developing reading and writing skills, and impressing upon them the value of saving our history for future generations.

Rick has two sons, Seneca and Dusty, and lives near Prineville, Oregon. He writes in a cabin in the timbered foothills of the Ochoco Mountains.